Mark DeVries has given us a very clear and readable rationale for rooting our youth ministry within the family structure. This will be one of those books that youth workers find they must read.

DUFFY ROBBINS
Chairman, Department of Youth Ministry, Eastern College

This important book by a seasoned minister to youth argues for a Christian approach to young people by way of families—nuclear and ecclesial—rather than pied pipers. It is thoughtful, suggestive and groundbreaking.

THOMAS W. GILLESPIE
President, Princeton Theological Seminary

This is the book we have been waiting for. Mark DeVries brings us a wealth and depth of understanding of the youth culture that few in America can provide. He is taking the necessary step of moving us from "traditional youth ministry" into a different style of youth work that is desperately needed.

JIM BURNS
President, National Institute of Youth Ministry

Family ministry as a concept is spreading rapidly throughout the youth ministry culture. Mark DeVries's work demonstrates that he has been and will continue to be a pioneer and pacesetter for that movement.

RICHARD DUNN
Chairman, Department of Youth Ministry, Trinity College

I appreciate Mark's thoroughness and desire to risk as well as venture into uncharted territory. Effective youth ministry has always begun in this way. I endorse his premise and support the idea that youth ministry is in a new day requiring new approaches.

CLIFF ANDERSON
Interim Director, Institute for Youth Ministry

Mark is absolutely right in his assessment of the direction youth ministry needs to go in the future. This is definitely one of the most important books on youth ministry that has ever been written.

WAYNE RICE
Co-founder, Youth Specialties

D1316752

Family-Based Youth Ministry

Reaching the Been-There, Done-That Generation

Mark DeVries

Foreword by Earl F. Palmer

INTERVARSITY PRESS
DOWNERS GROVE, ILLINOIS 60515

InterVarsity Press® is the book-publishing division of InterVarsity Christian Fellowship®, a student movement active on campus at hundreds of universities, colleges and schools of nursing in the United States of America, and a member movement of the International Fellowship of Evangelical Students. For information about local and regional activities, write Public Relations Dept., InterVarsity Christian Fellowship, 6400 Schroeder Rd., P.O. Box 7895, Madison, WI 53707-7895.

All Scripture quotations, unless otherwise indicated, are taken from the HOLY BIBLE, NEW INTERNATIONAL VERSION®. NIV®. Copyright ©1973, 1978, 1984 by International Bible Society. Used by permission of Zondervan Publishing House. All rights reserved.

Skit in appendix A is coauthored by Robert D. Wolgemuth and used with his permission.

Cover photograph: Jim Whitmer

ISBN 0-8308-1396-9

Printed in the United States of America ♾

Library of Congress Cataloging-in-Publication Data
DeVries, Mark.
  Family-based youth ministry: reaching the been-there, done-that generation/Mark DeVries.
    p.   cm.
  Includes bibliographical references.
  ISBN 0-8308-1396-9
  1. Church work with teenagers.   2. Christian education of teenagers.   I. Title.
  BV4447.D45   1994
  259'.23—dc20   94-28335
                                                                      CIP

15   14   13   12   11   10   9   8   7   6   5   4   3   2

04   03   02   01   00   99   98   97   96   95

To Susan,
who daily treats my trivia
as if it were the most important news in the world,
who lives with such infectious joy
that few can be with her long without laughing
and who has given me more in the past fifteen years
than most men receive in ten lifetimes.

• • • • • • • • • • • • • • • • • •

Acknowledgments

When I began this project, back in 1989, I would never have guessed how many different people would wind up adding their own unique contributions to my thinking about a new model for youth ministry. I'd like to thank

My Formative Family
☐ my parents—for the unparalleled influence you had in setting the course for my life as a Christian.
☐ my "bonus" parents (Richard, Louise and Caroline)—for embracing me as part of your own families.
☐ John, Gene, Jerry and all the other ministers (and minister wanna-bes) in my parents' families—no one was ever surrounded by as rich a cloud of witnesses.

My Pastors
☐ George and Trish Holland—for seeing through an obnoxious teenager and celebrating his gifts for ministry.
☐ Dick Freeman—for loving Jesus Christ with a contagious passion and for not firing me when I drove a 14-foot bus under the church's 13-foot carport.

☐ Don Childs—for letting a fly-by-night seminary student from another denomination practice on the kids in your church.

☐ Bill Bryant—for giving me the freedom to experiment in youth ministry and for setting a standard of excellence that motivated me to look beyond my own limited perspective.

My Mentors

☐ Robert Wolgemuth—for dragging us to Nashville, clinging to Christ when it would have been so simple to let go and giving us two of the greatest interns our church has ever seen. (Is it good?)

☐ Weldon and Barbara Walker—for your wise cousel through all those years when we were trying to figure out what we were going to do when we grow up.

☐ Steve Eyre—for reading Jonathan Edwards with me and convincing me that I really could write a book.

☐ Earl Palmer—for your vision for mentoring young pastors, eager love for learning and ability to bring out more in people than they ever knew was there (and for quoting C. S. Lewis as if you'd really been to Narnia almost every time you talk).

☐ Cindy "O Holy One" Bunch-Hotaling (IVP)—for laughing when I tried to be funny and giving invaluable suggestions about the manuscript. (Voicemail, anyone?)

☐ Dick Armstrong and Ron White—for letting me make up classes that didn't exist.

☐ The Mentors, the "Zookeepers" and other colleagues.

My Partners in Ministry

☐ Larry Coulter—for getting me into this whole book-writing thing in the first place and for spending a week with me in Princeton to get the ball rolling. (Time for a Thomas Sweet?)

☐ the Princeton Long-Term Youth Ministry Planning Team (Kendy Easley, Ron Scates, Robert Morris, Emily Anderson, Dale

Gillespie) for listening and giving me feedback on my Family-Based Youth Ministry seminar more times than we care to remember (sui generis!).

☐ Nan Russell, my teaching partner—for spending the past five years working the kinks out of our family-based curriculum and sharing your wild ride journey with me. (Please don't get arrested again—at least not in front of the teenagers!)

☐ Debbie and Kirk Freeman, Colyer and Drew Robison, Missy Wolgemuth, Ginger Yowell, Margaret Burnett, Chris Carson and Emmett and Spick—for your teachable spirits and the secret encouragement your receptivity gave to my thinking.

☐ the leaders, the Youth Committee, the YACs, the Parent's Club, the interns, the prayer partners, the mentors, my colleagues on the staff at First Presbyterian Church in Nashville—for creating the synergy that has become the means for God to do his surprising work among us here.

☐ Our Dear Friends (you know who you are)—for your random acts of kindness that have empowered us to see a glimmer of what lies beyond our own blinders.

☐ My Loyal Opponents (you know who *you* are too)—for challenging me to clarify my thinking and to broaden my perspective to include your point of view.

☐ Trish "I've got some good news and some bad news" Callison—for putting your life on hold to complete my incomplete footnotes. (Leslie and John thank you too.)

☐ my bride, Susan, and my three children, Adam ("Hoops? Yeah [yawn]. Great!"), Debbie (How about reading *this* book as a bedtime story?) and Leigh (the "Laughing Moderator")—for honoring me with your respect even when I deserve so much less.

• • • • • • • • • • • • • • • • • • •

Foreword

I remember hearing the youth pastor Mark DeVries from Nashville First Presbyterian Church speak at a seminar in which he shared with a roomful of pastors his vision for ministry to youth. I thought at the time that what he was telling us was both refreshing and vitally important for the ministry to and among youth to which we are called as Christians. Now I have read his book and I still feel the same way.

Mark DeVries takes youth seriously, and, therefore, he does not see the role of the youth pastor as a stepping stone to "larger" ministries or what might be thought of as more important appointments. He sees youth ministry as a totally significant post, just as pediatrics in medicine is not an entry level into medicine that later evolves toward the "more important" responsibility of geriatrics.

I think Mark DeVries and his new breed of youth pastors will be, in fact, youth workers all their lives wherever they are called to serve and in whatever use of their gifts to which the church lays claim, and as a result the church and youth and their families will be the better for it. This is because every one of us knows that churches die down like forests when they do not win the next generation to faith in Jesus Christ. The big question is: What is it that wins youth to faith and helps them to catch their stride as growing Christians? It is not playing at church. It is not unfocused programs to occupy their time. It is the good news of the person Jesus Christ. He is the most winsome fact that we have to share with any generation.

The question of durability and strategy for our ministry with youth is the focus of Mark's book, and he makes a profoundly important point as he argues that the most substantial ministry with the most long-lasting positive result is that ministry that relates to young men and women as members of families. This means we who do youth ministry are really involved in family ministry. The African saying puts it well, "It takes a village to raise a child," and the first village for every human being is the family of origin. Therefore, our ministry must encourage and strengthen that original village with friendly, nonexploitive adults for youth to borrow in their growing up and for families to borrow, too. I salute Pastor DeVries for this notable book which is a great gift to the church in helping us to know how to stand alongside youth and their families.

Earl F. Palmer

• • • • • • • • • • • • • • • • • • •

Introduction

Several years ago I heard the surprising news that my good friend Jim, an incredibly well-respected youth pastor in Texas, was leaving youth ministry. This guy was one of the most effective youth ministers I had ever known. He had over 200 teenagers meeting weekly in small discipleship groups and creative programming that drew young people from all over the city.

Certainly, there is nothing shocking about youth workers changing jobs. But I did wonder *why* Jim was quitting—and quitting not only his present position but youth ministry altogether. Did he get a better offer somewhere else? Was he moving on to become a "real" minister? Maybe he was going to start a profitable curriculum business? Make his own video series? I thought of all the possibilities, but his answer hit me cold.

"I am leaving," he said, "because I feel this overwhelming sense of failure."

"Sense of failure?" I was stunned. This man had been a model for me, someone whose ministry I was actively seeking to imitate.

And he tells me he feels like a failure? It just didn't make sense.

But since Jim left youth ministry, his words have begun to make more and more sense to me, and I am starting to see that his experience may actually be more the norm than the exception. In fact, as I talk with more and more "successful" youth ministers, I am seeing that almost every one suffers from a frustrating sense of failure. All have wondered more than once, "Am I really making any difference?"

Youth ministers know the anxiety a juggler feels keeping a knife, a bat and a fire stick in the air all at the same time. They know the temporary insanity required to move directly from suicide counseling into an egg roulette competition and then into teaching a group of teenagers who are not afraid to yawn in public. They know the nagging feeling of inadequacy that comes from always feeling like the runt of the litter on a church staff. And they've heard the not-so-silent whisperings, "Is he (or she) ever going to become a real minister?"

Youth ministers know that they must always hold their enthusiasm about their teenagers' testimonies with a grain of salt. They have heard too much from too many who didn't follow through on their words. They know the frustration of being called "disorganized" because they forgot to bring mustard for the otherwise perfect cookout. And they've fallen from the tightrope of listening to too much or too little criticism.

But whether from the call of God or from temporary insanity, they—and I—love this work. And even when things are at their worst, many of us still can't come up with anything else we'd rather do. Despite the nagging sense of frustration common to all of us, I've met very few youth workers who are out of ideas. Most are out of time, energy, patience and money. But ideas? We've got them by the truckload. Almost all of us know what we *ought* to be doing, but we just can't seem to keep all the youth ministry plates spinning at one time.

We would like to write great newsletter articles, prepare scintillating sermons, visit every kid in the group, boost attendance, work with parents, be available to handle crises at the drop of a hat, have a model family, keep praying and studying on our own, visit the schools regularly, disciple our volunteer leaders, train great teachers, find (or write!) curricula for Sunday school, build small groups, develop youth leadership, give stirring weekly reports, write letters to college students, teach guitar lessons, send personal birthday cards to each young person, involve youth in mission on a monthly basis, plan great retreats and monthly fun trips, promote and fill all the trips, collect money, fill the sanctuary with visible teenagers on Sunday morning, be the spiritual giant and fun-loving charisma machine we were hired to be, and of course *relax*—all at the same time!

But because we can't possible keep all the plates spinning, youth ministry at its best involves a continual process of setting and adjusting priorities—deciding what we will wring our hands about and what we will let slide. For most of us, ministry to or through parents of teenagers has simply been one of the many things on our "to do" list that we have had to "let slide."

Jim Burns tells the story of a recent Youth Specialties seminar on "The Family and Youth Ministry." In preparation for the seminar, the leader polled a number of successful youth ministers across the country. He asked, "What are you doing as a youth worker to help families succeed?" The overwhelming response was, "I believe it ought to be happening, but I just haven't gotten around to doing it."[1]

The ironic truth is that youth leaders may have at their fingertips the resource for vastly expanding the scope of their ministry. But many of us see this resource as something that "gets in the way" of youth ministry, and so we lay it aside. We are like the would-be handyman who attempts to move a boulder from his yard with a screwdriver, all the while complaining that the sledgehammer and the pickax keep getting in his way. He may or may not get the job done, but one thing is certain—he will soon be exhausted and frustrated.

This book is written for youth workers who are tired of quick fixes and easy answers. It is also written for anyone responsible for a Christian ministry to teenagers—pastors, youth committee members, parents, volunteer leaders and search committees looking for youth pastors. It is written for parents who want to understand the forces that most significantly impact their children's spiritual formation.

As the title suggests, this is also a book about families. Let me tip my hand a little. One of my working assumptions is that the contemporary crisis in youth ministry has little to do with programming and everything to do with families. Our culture has put an incredible amount of emotional weight on the shoulders of the nuclear family, a weight which I believe families were never intended to bear alone. One of the secrets to a lasting ministry with teenagers is to find ways to undergird nuclear families with the rich support of the extended Christian family of the church and for these two formative families to work together in leading young people toward mature Christian adulthood.

This book gives the rationale for a paradigm shift in our approach to working with teenagers. I want to challenge some of the assumptions underlying the way it has "always" been done and give an alternative approach. The first few chapters will identify what I see as the core deficiency in traditional youth ministry. Most of the book is dedicated to offering a realistic, informed understanding of the factors that lead teenagers to Christian maturity, so that churches can be helped in providing them with a ministry that lasts for the long haul. To that end I have provided a section at the end of each chapter called "Implications for Ministry." These ideas will give some practical handles for the application of the principles outlined in each chapter. In addition there is a smorgasbord of suggestions in the final chapter.

This is a book about a new way of approaching youth ministry that goes beyond the traditional formulas that seem, inherently, to set up youth leaders for failure. But this is not a "Shell Answer Man" handbook. You will not find in these pages the silver bullet to make ministry to teenagers a snap; working with youth will never be easy. What you *will* find is an approach that can vastly expand the long-term effectiveness of any Christian ministry to teenagers.

It's disturbing how few Christian teenagers actually grow toward a more mature Christian faith. A national study by Search Institute found that, in general, teenagers' church involvement and faith stagnate during high school.

JAY KESLER, *Energizing Your Teenager's Faith*

The decade of the 1980s has drawn to a close and the health of ministries to high-school students in the United States is less than exciting. For the most part ministries which employ youth specialists are locked within the white middle class, as church boards urged by parents attempt to ensure the passing of Christian values from one generation to the next. . . . Parachurch agencies which attempt to reach the entire student population with a single strategy have ceased to grow.

MARK SENTER, *The Coming Revolution in Youth Ministry*

I have spent the past seventeen years working with youth toward one principal goal: to see a personal faith in Jesus Christ become the controlling reality in kids' lives. According to some standards for measuring success, my seventeen-year investment may be viewed as relatively ineffective. Although it is impossible to know what the long-term impact of my involvement in kids' lives really will be, at this time I can point to only small handfuls of kids and young adults with whom I have worked who bear the marks of being controlled by a personal faith in Christ. Though the personal rewards and joys of working with kids have been tremendous, these seventeen years have made one thing clear: Personal faith in Christ cannot be mass produced in adolescents' lives.

KEVIN HUGGINS, *Parenting Adolescents*

What the whole church must face—local congregations and parachurch ministries alike—is the enormity of the need. The facts speak for themselves: only 15 to 20 percent of American teenagers are significantly involved in a church.

DOUG BURLEIGH, past president of Young Life

1
Something's Wrong
The Crisis in Traditional Youth Ministry

Traditional" *youth ministry: it sounds like an oxymoron in a day* when youth ministries pride themselves on being outrageous, wild, out of control—anything but "traditional." But in the 1990s, such a clear pattern for youth ministry has emerged that no term describes it quite so well as "traditional."

⌈What I am calling "traditional youth ministry" has little to do with style or programming or personality. It has to do with the place of teenagers in the community of faith. Over the last century, churches and parachurch youth ministries alike have increasingly (and often unwittingly) held to a single strategy that has become the most common characteristic of this model: the isolation of teenagers from the adult world and particularly from their own parents.⌋

This traditional model has its roots in the turn of the century with the rise of the Christian Endeavor Movement, a church-based, interdenominational program created especially for youth. Undergirded by a culture in which teenagers had frequent interaction with adults and with their own parents, Christian Endeavor (and church imitations that followed it) flourished. Using a Sunday-night meeting format, these Christian Endeavor-type programs had discovered a creative model for reaching teenagers.

When the popularity of the Sunday-night Christian Endeavor format began to wane in the 1940s, a new style of youth ministry was launched. The Young Life and Youth for Christ organizations hit on the strategy of reaching young people apart from the traditional church setting. Over the next few decades these ministries expanded with explosive energy and reached scores of teenagers whom the institutional church seemed to be missing.

In the last twenty-five years, groups like Youth Specialties have popularized the parachurch style of youth ministry by marketing their ideas to local churches. As a result, the face of youth ministry in the nineties has become increasingly creative, with a plethora of products designed to reach teenagers more effectively. But despite these external improvements, contemporary youth ministry is in crisis.

I was speaking at a conference recently and was asked to give a thirty-second explanation of my seminar on family-based youth ministry. I reported what I have heard from many youth workers over the past five years: "What worked five or ten years ago with teenagers is just not working anymore." I was not surprised to see the nods of agreement from the youth ministry professionals in this group.

Later on that evening, one of the conference participants pulled me aside and made a telling remark: "I agree that the things I did five years ago don't work anymore. But the real shock for me is that the things I did five months ago aren't working anymore either!"

Success: Mature Christian Teenagers?

The stereotypical guitar-playing youth leader with a set of ideas books and a floppy Bible is no longer enough to attract the attention and enthusiasm of our youth. Long-term youth ministers who have followed the futures of their youth group members have begun to sense intuitively that something is wrong. Most veteran youth ministers I know have a busload of stories like my story about Jenny.

As a seventh-grader, Jenny began visiting our youth group with a friend during church basketball season. Quite honestly, I expected that she would disappear after the ten-game season was over. But was I ever wrong! At some point during that first year, Jenny responded to the claims of Christ and became a model youth group member. She was a regular fixture at our Sunday-morning, Sunday-evening and Wednesday-night youth programs. She sat in the youth section in worship and even showed up when missionaries gave their slide shows ("India—Land of Contrast" [B-e-e-p]).

Jenny came from a family in which the Christian faith was irrelevant at best. Her parents were supportive of her involvement in the church, but they made it clear that Jenny's spiritual priorities were not for them. But, in spite of her family situation, we had reached Jenny.

Whenever I had doubts about whether our ministry was having any impact, I would remind myself of Jenny and her amazing story. If anyone bore the marks of the success of our ministry, it was she. Like most youth ministers, I had trouble evaluating the success of our program strictly on the basis of how large a crowd we could gather for youth meetings. But Jenny's story gave me something to hang on to. I could point to her when I needed assurance that I was actually doing something right.

As Jenny grew older, I became more enthusiastic as I watched her precocious spiritual maturity develop. By the time she was a sophomore, she was a part of our student leadership team and someone I held up as a model for the younger members of our youth group. By anyone's standards, we had succeeded with Jenny. She was a mature Christian teenager, well ahead of most of her peers who grew up in Christian homes.

I left for seminary just before Jenny's junior year. That same year she moved away as well. I lost touch with her for several years; so when one of our mutual friends mentioned seeing her, I was anxious to hear how she had grown.

Jenny is currently not active in any church. Apparently, after leaving our active youth ministry, she had not been impressed with any of the churches in her new city and chose not to get involved in any of them. She has graduated from college and, after living with her boyfriend for a while, is now on the fast track toward success in her career. Although she looks back on her youth group experience nostalgically, she has shown little interest in pursuing her faith as an adult.

I haven't closed the book on Jenny's story. I continue to pray for her, trusting that God who began his good work will bring it to completion. But if Jenny's story has shown me one thing, it is that something was wrong with the way I was measuring success.

The important aspect of Jenny's story is that our program *succeeded* in leading her to become a mature Christian *teenager,* but somehow failed to place her on the track toward mature Christian *adulthood.* We were short-sighted, focusing on the short-term objective of keeping her involved and growing but forgetting the long-term goal of laying a foundation that would last.

There is little doubt that there are more "successful" youth ministries today than there were twenty years ago. But what are the long-term results of youth ministries?

George Barna's research indicates that "since 1970, there has been no appreciable change in the proportion of adults who attend church services at any given time during the week."[1] The Lilly Foundation discovered that 40 percent of those who were confirmed in the 1950s and early 1960s "no longer belong to a church or attend church regularly, yet still consider themselves to be religious."[2]

William Willimon and Robert Wilson describe this crisis from the perspective of the United Methodist Church. They target their denomination's "inability to retain . . . young people, after their maturity, in the church" as one of the chief causes of decline in their denomination.[3]

The struggles in my own denomination, the Presbyterian Church (U.S.A.), are symptomatic of the crisis in other mainline churches, all of which have had increasing difficulty "hanging on" to their youth once they become adults.

Tom Gillespie, president of Princeton Seminary, has pinpointed this problem:

> The truth of the matter is that the chief cause of our membership decline is our inability over the past quarter of a century to translate our faith to our children. Put simply, we are unable to keep our children in the church when they become adults. As a result, we are not only a dwindling church but an aging church as well.[4]

Most young people who disaffiliate with the church do so by the time they have become sixteen years old. Research confirms that those youth who drop out of the church do so not when they leave for college, as is often assumed, but while they are still in high school.[5]

The crisis in youth ministry continues in spite of the exponential growth in the amount of money being spent on youth ministry and the number of professionals employed to do this work. "Successful" youth ministries do not necessarily produce mature Christian adults.

Wanted: Mature Christian Adults

This crisis cannot be addressed simply by making increased efforts in evangelism. Many programs are growing. The crisis is that we are not leading teenagers to *mature Christian adulthood.* I have found chart 1 to be a helpful starting point as a contrast

Chart 1. Comparison of Childhood Faith and Mature Adult Faith[6]

Childhood Faith	Mature Adult Faith
Good Christians don't have pain or disappointment.	God uses our pain and disappointment to make us better Christians.
God helps those who help themselves.	God helps those who admit their own helplessness.
God wants to make us happy.	God wants to make us into the image of Jesus.
Faith will help us always explain what God is doing (things always work out).	Faith helps us stand under God's sovereignty even when we have no idea what God is doing.
The closer we get to God, the more perfect we become.	The closer we get to God, the more we become aware of our own sinfulness.
Mature Christians have answers.	Mature Christians can wrestle honestly with tough questions because we trust that God has the answers.
Good Christians are always strong.	Our strength is in admitting our weakness.
We go to church because our friends are there, we have great leaders, and we get something out of it.	We go to church because we belong to the body of Christ.

between the kinds of attitudes we hope our youth will grow out of and those we hope they will grow into.

If our youth programs are well attended, it is easy for youth leaders (and churches) to be satisfied with the attitudes of childish faith. But the attitudes of spiritual maturity cannot be mass-produced in teens' lives. These attitudes are created as young people move out of the comfortable bubble of the youth program and live out their faith through the challenging and often monotonous experiences of life.

Jim Rayburn, the founder of Young Life, is frequently quoted as saying, "It's a sin to bore a kid." I think I understand what he is getting at (that is, the traditional structures of the church can often be obstacles rather than windows through which we see Christ). But keeping teenagers from ever being bored in their faith can actually deprive them of opportunities to develop the discipline and perseverance needed to live the Christian life. It might be more of a sin to suggest to young people that the Christian life is always fun and never boring. It is precisely in those experiences that teenagers might describe as "boring" that Christian character is often formed.

Christian faith may begin on the mountaintop, but Christian character is formed in the crucible of pain. We should not be shocked, then, to discover that the depth of faith maturity among Christians in our country pales in comparison to that of Christians who have lived out their faith under the shadow of persecution.

Mature Christian adults, then, are those people who no longer depend on "whistles and bells" to motivate them to live out their faith. They have become proactive Christians—not reactive. When young people grow up to be *reactive* Christian adults, they are constantly waiting for someone or something to attract them, to involve them, to impress them. A reactive Christian puts the responsibility for his spiritual life on someone else.

If our programs are training teenagers to be reactive, immature Christians, we can expect those young people eventually to become discouraged by the difficulty and boredom of the Christian life. Could it be that the majority of our efforts in programming and publicity may, in fact, be moving teens away from rather than toward mature Christian adulthood?

The Right Numbers

What a great night it had been! It seemed like young people were crammed into every corner of the room. We had pulled out all the stops for this first Sunday night after Easter. For the first time in my six years at this church we had over 100 young people together. Parents and church colleagues patted me on the back, and I drove home satisfied that we had finally begun to get this program off the ground. But even as I breathed a satisfied sigh of self-congratulation, a vague uneasiness came over me.

I began to wonder, "What was Jesus feeling when the crowd gathered on Palm Sunday, less than a week before his death? Was he thrilled by the attendance and their enthusiasm, or could he see through the crowd to what they were already in the process of becoming? What do numbers really tell us anyway?"

We may live in a culture in which bigger has become synonymous with better, but we serve a Lord who spoke of his kingdom in terms of a mustard seed, a widow's mite and a single lost sheep. I love building a crowd. It makes me feel good. It makes me look good. And because of what building a crowd does for me, I have often mistaken short-term success for long-term effectiveness.

The short-sighted standard of success of traditional youth ministry reminds me of a "Hagar the Horrible" cartoon. Hagar has his men in a Viking ship rowing with all their might, but they are in complete confusion. After several frames, they finally begin to stroke together. In the next to the last frame, Hagar is praising the men, "You've finally gotten it! Now we're going somewhere!" The final frame shows the enthusiastic group of soldiers rowing themselves off the edge of the earth. Ultimately, Hagar didn't know where he was leading his group, but he was proud of the fact that they were making such good progress.

As ironic as it may sound, my complaint is not that we are too concerned with numbers but that we don't take numbers seriously enough. Avoidance of numbers certainly is not characteristic of the New Testament writers. Jesus knew exactly how many disciples he had. Often they are referred to not as "the disciples" but simply as "the twelve." Jesus sent out seventy disciples to minister; over 4000 people were fed miraculously at one event and over 5000 at another. Luke tells us that in the early days of the church 3000 were saved in a single day. Paul reminds us that Jesus appeared to over 500 after his resurrection. And the shepherd in Jesus' parable knew the exact number of sheep he was charged to take care of.

As biblical Christians, we do not need to be embarrassed about using numbers. But frequently youth workers and churches evaluate their success or failure by the *wrong* numbers.

I interviewed the pastor of a small church recently. I could tell by the tone in his voice that he felt their youth ministry was a failure. He expressed his disappointment about their youth program—how hard it was to get teenagers to come, how few of their youth programs had actually worked, and so on. I asked about his numbers, and he explained that the church had eighteen young people, and of that group, fifteen were involved in the life of the church *every week!* The pastor, somewhat embarrassed, explained that most of their involvement was not with other youth but with adults in the church. He evaluated his youth ministry as unsuccessful because he couldn't get roomfuls of teens together for a youth meeting.

On the same day I visited a church in the same city that had over 10,000 members. I spoke to its youth minister as he was on his way out the door and only had time to ask him a few questions, so of course I asked about numbers. "How many young people do you have in your group?"

"About 200," he responded, without an ounce of arrogance, but with an obvious air of success.

"And how many students are on your rolls?"

"About 400." He hesitated and went on. "We have decided that the best way to build our group is to have about twice as many on the rolls as we expect to see come. We spend our time with the ones that show up. It *works*."

Both of these youth leaders were looking at the wrong numbers. The one who had fifteen out of eighteen involved weekly felt like a failure because he did not have many teens attending youth meetings. And the youth worker whose ministry was essentially ignoring "about 200" students felt like a success, simply because of the size of the group.

The ironic fact for most of us is that we spend huge amounts of energy getting *more* teens involved while ignoring most of the ones God has already given us. It is no coincidence that once Jesus chose the twelve (the ones for whom he would be responsible), he didn't go out looking for more!

The Search for New Models

Mark Senter, in his comprehensive history of youth ministry in the United States, suggests that every fifty years one or two major youth ministry agencies are recognized as the pacesetters for that era. Although the history does not fall out into exactly fifty-year stages, Senter traces a definite pattern that can help us understand the current state of youth ministry in the U.S.

1830s—1850s: Sunday School Union and Young Men's Christian Organization
1890s: Society for Christian Endeavor
1940s: Youth for Christ and Young Life
1990s: ????

Not only does Senter identify an approximately fifty-year pattern between stages, he also documents a clear pattern within each stage. Each of these movements was carried along for the first twenty or thirty years by a wave of excitement and constant innovation. By the thirty-year point, each began to become institutionalized, its strategies codified into planning manuals and many of its methods adopted by the church. By the end of the fifty years, the once cutting-edge ministries had become tame institutions, and the stage was set for a new movement to begin.

If Senter is right (and I think he is), the stage is now set for a new movement to lead the way in the next youth ministry cycle. The shape of youth ministry is in transition across the United States. The Young Life and Youth for Christ ministries have both had significant turnover in the senior leadership (for example, both have had new presidents in the last ten years). Although teens in some locations are attending these groups in record numbers, these parachurch group have themselves become institutions whose growth has leveled off.[7]

Senter explains,

A study of history suggests we are about to see a fundamental departure from what we have understood to be youth ministry during the closing decades of the twentieth century. Though most parachurch agencies and denominational programs will continue to exist and make contributions, . . . their strategies have become flawed. . . . A new movement is about to appear and may already be emerging.[8]

Mike Yaconelli, in a recent address at the National Youth Workers Convention, seemed to be suggesting the same thing:

> Kids today are unlike any other generation of kids we've ever had to work with in youth ministry. All of the techniques, all of the strategies, all of the philosophies that we all are using and grew up with don't work any more. But if we don't wake up in the church and begin to radically alter and change what it is that we're doing with kids, we've lost them. . . .
>
> We need some radical new models for ministering to kids, and we'd better wake up to the fact that if we don't, we've lost these kids. [9]

Don Griggs, responding to the 1990 findings of the Search Institute report, has suggested, "New models must be developed for Christian education—models that focus on adults and senior highs and that are offered at times other than Sunday morning."[10]

Traditional youth ministry in the church today may have become little more than a hodgepodge of the structural remains of youth ministry dinosaurs. Every church has a youth Sunday-school program. Why? Because every church has "always" had a youth Sunday-school program. Almost every church also has a Sunday-night youth program. Why? Because we can't seem to let go of the Christian Endeavor structure that worked so well at the beginning of the 1900s. And nearly every church youth ministry has developed a fragmented collection of parachurch resources and ideas about youth discipleship groups, special events, mission trips, and so on.

The next stage of youth ministry will not be found by returning to any of these structures. The answer to the crisis in youth ministry does not lie in infusing our tired structures with life. We need an entirely new way of looking at youth ministry.

Implications for Ministry

1. Now, more than ever, churches need to concentrate on num-

bers, making every effort to be faithful in providing a ministry to the students God has given to the church.

2. Because faith maturity develops as young people are engaged in their faith, churches can work to provide all their teenagers with ministries of their own.

3. Realistically, only a limited number of teenagers can be given leadership in the youth program. But most teenagers can be given a ministry alongside an adult in the church, a ministry that benefits someone other than the youth.

Wild Hair—These are years for bold experimentation in youth ministry. Churches should not be afraid to step back from some of the sacred structures of Sunday school and youth group in order to develop a ministry to teenagers that is clearly designed to build long-term faith maturity. At the end of each chapter I will give one "Wild Hair" idea for those churches willing and able to step radically away from what is expected.

• • • • • • • • • • • • • • • • •

The thing that impresses me most about America is the way parents obey their children.

EDWARD, *Duke of Windsor (1895-1977)*

Adolescence has become a waiting period of enforced leisure with few responsibilities and little or no meaningful contact with adults.

"Adolescent Rolelessness in Modern Society," *a report of the Carnegie Council on Adolescent Development*

Ours is the only era in the entire history of human life on this planet in which the "elders" of the tribe ask its newer members what the tribal rules and standards of expected behavior would be.

PAUL RAMSEY, *ethicist, Princeton University*

More often than not, children are learning major value systems in life from the horizontal peer-culture. The vertical structure is not there in adequate increments of time or intensity to do the job.

GORDON MACDONALD, *The Effective Father*

When peers have dialogue primarily with peers, they fail to be exposed to those with more advanced insights and more highly developed faculties. . . . Our children, who are constantly engrossed in peer-centered activities, interact minimally with those more mature than themselves.

STEPHEN GLENN and JANE NELSEN, *Raising Self-Reliant Children in a Self-Indulgent World*

The culture of the electronic media prescribes perpetual adolescence and consumption as developmental ideals. Indeed, perpetual adolescence and consumption constitute the twin-pronged gospel of these media.

QUENTIN J. SCHULTZE et al., *Dancing in the Dark*

• • • • • • • • • • • • • • • •

2
Is Anybody
Out There?
The Growth of
Teenage Isolation

Teenagers today are in trouble. And what they don't know can literally kill them. Our culture sends its kids into adulthood ill-prepared for the increasing demands of our complex society. Like so many children in the Middle East who defend themselves by throwing rocks at soldiers with machine guns, this generation of kids enters the confusing battleground of adulthood armed with nothing more than vague values and innocuous religious experiences.

As in any war, there have been casualties. Teenagers are dying at a higher rate than they were thirty years ago—victims of accidents, suicide, homicide, drugs and alcohol. While the members of every other age group are more likely to *live* than they were thirty years ago, adolescence has become for many a life-and-death obstacle course.

Most of us who work with teenagers have heard the negative

statistics. But we don't have to read them to know they are true. We are not surprised to learn that the number of teenagers committed to institutions in the last decade has risen by 400 percent,[1] or that in 1985 53,000 teenagers died in the United States (by comparison, 56,000 Americans died in five years of war in Vietnam).[2]

We work with the teenage boy who has been in and out of rehabilitation three times. We visit the hospital where one of our college girls rotated comatose on a board for months because of an accident after drinking at a fraternity party. We've stood beside enough graves to know that something is very wrong.

Social scientists and armchair politicians all seem to have their explanations—from the deterioration of public education to the breakdown of the American family. Without a doubt, no single factor is entirely responsible for the frightening situation faced by our teenagers. But I believe a single trend in our culture has, more than any other factor, precipitated the crisis. Until we take this trend seriously, our ministry to young people will be severely limited in its impact.

Arenas of Isolation

In a recent research project, a group of seventy-five suburban teenagers were given beepers and belts and asked to write down exactly what they were doing and feeling at the exact moment the beeper sounded. After several months of observation, the results gave a portrait of how teens spend their time. The single most disturbing conclusion, as recorded in the book *Being Adolescent,* was the unprecedented neglect of teenagers by adults. The study documented the very large amount of time that teenagers spend alone and the dangerously limited contact they actually have with adults.[3]

Teenagers are increasingly isolated from the adult world. And even when young people are "with" adults, it is usually in a large group setting in which the teenagers are being entertained, informed or directed by those adults, leaving little opportunity for the dialogue and collaboration required for youth to learn adult values.

Cornell University's Urie Bronfenbrenner cites nine specific changes that have taken place during the past generation which have increasingly separated children and youth from the world of adults, especially the adults in their own families:

1. fathers' vocational choices which remove them from the home for lengthy periods of time

2. an increase in the number of working mothers

3. a critical escalation in the divorce rate

4. a rapid increase in single-parent families

5. a steady decline in the extended family

6. the evolution of the physical environment of the home (family rooms, playrooms and master bedrooms)

7. the replacement of adults by the peer group

8. the isolation of children from the work world

9. the insulation of schools from the rest of society

This last factor has caused Bronfenbrenner to describe the current U.S. educational system as "one of the most potent breeding grounds for alienation in American society."[4] When he wrote these words in 1974, this trend toward isolation was in full swing, and it has not been significantly checked since that time.

In neighborhoods, schools, social activities, their own families and even at church, young people are afforded less and less opportunity to be with adults.

Neighborhoods

To begin with, consider the mere physical changes in neighborhoods over the past generation. Many of the newer subdivisions have sidewalks that connect each house only to its *own* driveway. Few neighborhoods today still have even the visible connection of sidewalks between neighbors.

I grew up in a Presbyterian manse. Next door to our home was Mr. Flanders's Schwinn bike shop. When I had nothing to do (which was often), I would travel the sidewalk over to Mr. Flanders's shop and look at his coin collections or run my fingers over the new bikes. Honestly, I don't remember one thing he ever said to me, but I do remember he was someone who let me peek into what it was like to be an adult. I was not close to Mr. Flanders; he was not a mentor. But he was a part of my developmental landscape—an entree into the adult world. Children and teenagers in our culture are more and more removed from this kind of adult—an adult to know "for free," not a tutor or a teacher or a parent or a babysitter or even a youth leader.

Many children have their schedules so packed that even if adults were available there would be little opportunity to spend time with them. From organized sports leagues to the growing amount of homework many schools are giving, teens have little time to do anything but check their schedules and run. Most young people grow up in neighborhoods populated by wandering children and dogs but very few visible adults. Sadly enough, the closest thing some children have to an available adult is 911.

Schools

Schools too have increasingly isolated junior-high and high-school students from the adult world. In some schools, teachers now have classes with as many as forty students. With the classes and teachers changing every fifty minutes, it is rare—if not impossible—for the average student to have any individual time to talk with his or her teachers.

Schools are no longer a place in which the less mature have the opportunity to interact with the more mature. Students are intentionally stratified to limit class groupings to only those within a certain range of ability. This horizontal peer structure may be seen as a more efficient way to teach, but this pattern prevents youth from developing the vertical relationships that will promote their maturity.

A growing number of very committed teachers have a tremendous impact on the values of their students. But as a general rule, teachers simply don't have time for nondirective conversations with their students. The majority of the time teenagers spend in school is dedicated to isolated work alone and periodically with peers, but seldom in meaningful conversation with adults.

Social Activities

Teenagers are also increasingly "on their own" when it comes to choosing social activities. From Pulaski, Tennessee, to New York, New York, resident teenagers complain that there is "nothing to do."

"Hanging out" with friends or partying in an adult-free home has become the norm of teenage social life. At one such party, a fight broke out between kids from rival high schools. In the process a high-school boy was stabbed and subsequently died. The parents who hosted the party were asked, "Where were you that evening?"

Their answer gives us a telling metaphor. They said, "We were upstairs. We just didn't want to get in the kids' way." When adults choose to "stay out of the kids' way," the consequences can be fatal.

When I was a college student, fifteen years ago, my friends and I discovered an unusual place where children and teenagers could "try on" being adults. On Friday nights, we would load up in my 1962 VW bug and drive twenty miles to the American Legion Hall in Elk, Texas. Every Friday night they had "kicker" (country-western) dancing. None of us liked the music much, but it was such a refreshing break from the pizza and movie monotony that we kept coming back month after month.

As I look back, I see now that Elk was one of the few places we could find eighty-year-old sweethearts and eight-year-old puppy lovers having fun together. There may still be some places like Elk, Texas, where our kids can go for fun, but I'm hard pressed to think of one.

Families

Without question, the most damaging isolation that teenagers in our culture experience is from their own families. American parents spend less time with their children than do parents in any other country in the world, according to Harvard psychiatrist Armand Nicholi. Fifty years ago, families worked and ate together by necessity. Teenagers and parents spent hours and hours together; in the process, young people could not avoid observing and listening in on the adult world. These experiences laid a natural track for adolescents to enter adulthood.

As families prospered, they no longer found it necessary to work and eat together. The natural bridge from childhood to adulthood was severely weakened, if not removed altogether. With one in four young people now indicating that they have *never* had a meaningful conversation with their father,[5] is it any wonder that 76 percent of the 1,200 teens surveyed in *USA Today* actually *want* their parents to spend more time with them?[6]

Andree Aließon Brooks, a *New York Times* journalist, in her eye-opening book *Children of Fast-Track Parents*, describes her interviews with scores of children and parents who seemed to "have it all": "If there was one theme that constantly emerged from my conversations with the children it was a surprising undercurrent of aloneness—feelings of isolation from peers as well as parents despite their busy lives."[7]

The Church

It might be hoped that churches would stand in the gap and provide an environment in which children and youth could dialogue and collaborate with adults. But sadly enough, for many teenagers, the place they are the most segregated from the world of adults is their church. And churches with the more "successful" youth programs seem to particularly exacerbate this problem.

Most "successful" youth ministries have their own youth Sunday school, youth missions, youth small groups, youth evangelism teams, youth worship, youth budget, youth interns, youth committees, youth offering, youth Bible studies, youth "elders" (never did understand that one), youth centers, youth choir, youth rooms, youth discipleship programs, youth conferences, youth retreats, youth fundraisers and (my personal favorite) youth ministers.

Even when families do worship together, almost inevitably the parents sit together, the children are shuffled off to "children's church," and the youth sit in the balcony. The church is the one place where teenagers could logically be linked to the world of adults, but for the most part, we have missed the opportunity.

Stuart Cummings-Bond has creatively referred to this isolation as a "one-eared Mickey Mouse." He uses figure 1 to describe how, in most churches, the program of the church and the youth ministry make only tangential contact.

I grew up in a small church whose youth program was a "failure" most of the time. Because our small Presbyterian church could never hang on to its part-time Baptist youth direc-

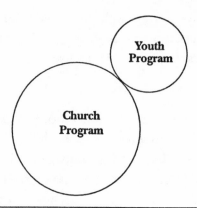

Figure 1. The One-Eared Mickey Mouse[8]

tors for very long, the pastor and the older members of the congregation had to spend a lot of time with the youth. In our sporadic youth group meetings, we played a lot of football, talked about sex more than once and had more lock-ins than I care to count.

But because the youth program was so inconsistent, we were forced to be involved with the adults in the church. We were bored to tears in worship. But, as a whole, almost every teenager in our youth group was in church every week. There was a clear sense of belonging to that place for *every* teenager in the church.

Our little church wasn't successful enough in its youth ministry to experience the "one-eared Mickey Mouse" phenomenon. But through my relationship with the pastor and even in the "boring worship service," I saw and heard the gospel. As a matter of fact, it was in this church, after our typically mediocre "Youth Sunday," that an elderly woman, Edna Lou Sullivan, pulled me aside and said, "Honey, you are going to be a minister someday." Fifteen years later, I still consider her words one of the first steps in my call to the ministry.

The less capable the church is at programming, the more

responsibility the youth themselves will be required to take. There are worse things a church can do to its teenagers than providing miserable programs for them—patently isolating teenagers from Christian adults is at the top of the list.

Mechanic or Surgeon?
Churches that use the traditional model for youth ministry approach the task of working with teenagers much like a mechanic would. When a mechanic sees a problem in an engine, he isolates the problem, and then he fixes it.

When leaders in churches around the United States began to see teenagers' growing disinterest with the church, they responded like a good mechanic: isolate and fix. Church leaders assumed that by isolating the youth department into its own independent subgroup in the church, they would instill all the values necessary for youth to grow to mature Christian adulthood. But the Christian community is not like a machine. This problem cannot be solved by isolation. As a matter of fact, this solution may have been worse than the original problem.

Because teenagers are an integral part of the *body* of Christ, we need to understand this problem as a physician would. When an organ is removed from a living body, that organ dies, and sometimes the body dies along with it. The same principle is true in the body of Christ. Whatever new models for youth ministry we develop must take seriously the fact that teenagers grow toward mature Christian adulthood as they are connected to the total body of Christ, not isolated from it.

Implications for Ministry
1. Try to go one month without isolating teenagers from the rest of the church. Instead, integrate them with adults in every typical youth ministry setting—youth could join different adult Sunday-

school classes or an adult small group, help in the nursery and help teach the children's classes.

2. Leaders could learn a great deal simply by finding out how many and which adults their teenagers spend their time with. A simple survey at the beginning of class, asking kids to list every adult they talked with over the past month and how long they spent talking, would be an informative tool for youth leaders.

3. Establish a task force to determine ways that the church can provide more opportunities for the teenagers in the church to build relationships with adults in the church. Choose three priorities for the coming year and implement them.

Wild Hair—Instead of youth group one night, assign the kids the job of having a half-hour visit with some adult outside of their family. Wait to have youth group again until all the visits have been made.

•   •   •   •   •   •   •   •   •   •   •   •   •   •   •   •   •   •   •

Lack of dialogue and collaboration between the more mature and less mature threatens the bonds of closeness, trust, dignity, and respect that hold our society together. . . . People are basically tribal creatures. Human beings have never done well in isolation.

STEPHEN GLENN and JANE NELSEN, *Raising Self-Reliant Children in a Self-Indulgent World*

Dick Clark's longevity as the premier impresario of rock is a symbol of rock's Peter Pan myth of eternal youth. The sight and sound of the Beach Boys (*Boys?* These guys are almost ready for Social Security) pretending they still belong on the beach impressing the young bimbos is an embodiment of the Romantic myth of youth.

KEN MYERS, *All God's Children and Blue Suede Shoes*

Never forget that the children of over-committed, harassed, exhausted parents are sitting ducks for the con men of our time.

JAMES DOBSON, *Children at Risk*

The young are in character prone to desire and ready to carry any desire they may have formed into action. Of bodily desires, it is the sexual to which they are most disposed to give way, and in regard to sexual desire they exercise no self-restraint. They are changeful too, and fickle in their desires, which are as transitory as they are vehement; for their wishes are keen without being permanent, like a sick man's fits of hunger and thirst.

ARISTOTLE, *4th century B.C.*

The inattention to children by our society poses a greater threat to our safety, harmony and productivity than any external enemy.

MARIAN WRIGHT EDELMAN, *Children's Defense Fund*

In a way it's a good thing adults don't know much about teens. If they knew all about us, they'd puke.

FOURTEEN-YEAR-OLD STUDENT quoted in the *Chicago Tribune*

3
The Developmental Disaster
The Impact of Teenage Isolation

O ne of the summer highlights for our Texas youth group was an annual New Braunfuls tubing trip. Aside from having to load fifty inflated inner tubes onto the top of the church bus, I loved everything about this trip. I actually enjoyed being thrown down the river chute with the kids. And I loved ending the day with the three-mile float downriver.

But between the chute and the "floating" parts of the trip, every tuber had to go over a simple three-foot waterfall. Most were thrown head over heels into the water, gasping between squeals of laughter. But those that weren't thrown from their tubes found themselves in an even more frustrating situation: they got stuck at the bottom of the falls.

It might take a physicist to explain why, but somehow the falls created a current that made it nearly impossible to paddle away. No matter how vigorously the people in the tubes paddled, the current would pull them back toward the falls.

I was almost always fortunate enough to be thrown from my tube; so I watched our group with enjoyment each time they attempted to gather on the other side of the falls for our day-ending float. Those who stayed in their tubes frantically paddled away from the falls, only to be immediately sucked right back in. The peculiar current of that place kept people stuck, unable to move forward. Unless they got out of their tubes or someone from outside the current helped them, there was simply no way out.

I can think of no better image for the way our culture causes young people to become "stuck" developmentally. Paddle as they might to move away from childhood, the current of their own culture pulls them back, keeping them tied to an immature, dependent lifestyle.

The U.S. Census Bureau confirms the increasing difficulty that young adults are having becoming independent. During the 1980s, more than half (54 percent) of adults between the ages of 18 and 24 were still living at home (up from 47 percent in 1970). In addition, more than one in ten adults between the ages of 25 and 34 were still at home, compared to 8 percent in 1970.[1]

The bridge from childhood to adulthood is getting longer and longer. Young people in our time are stuck in a peer-centered culture. And unless they can find the footing to step out of that culture, they will be perpetually stuck in adolescence.

Imagine what would happen if a group of inexperienced junior-highers were given the task of teaching each other how to scuba dive. One boy could argue that he understands how it is done—he's seen it a hundred times on television. One of the girls might remember a book about sea explorers she checked out in the third grade. And a third person might brag that he has the entire *Sea Hunt* series on videocassette. They might even all agree that one or more of them know what they are talking about. But if they actually attempted to teach each other to scuba dive, the consequences could be fatal.

Teenagers will not learn the skills required of mature adults in a peer-centered youth Sunday-school class. They will not learn these skills by talking with their friends. The process occurs as the less mature repeatedly have the opportunity to observe, dialogue and collaborate with the more mature. By denying teenagers opportunities for this kind of involvement with adults, our culture sends many youth into the "adult" years relationally, mentally and morally unprepared for the challenges of adulthood.

Relational Retardation

A film producer recently described the crisis among today's youth in this way:

> For too long, young people have been told that their greatest problems are drugs, sex, alcohol, etc. . . . These are, in fact, only symptoms of a much greater disease. The disease of youth is [that key relationships] are in disarray—their relationships with God, self, parents, friends, and the world.[2]

The movie *The Breakfast Club* gives a clue to the cause of this "disease" in relationships. In the movie, a group of mismatched teenagers are all serving detention together on a Saturday morning. There are no adults with significant parts in the movie.

After some uncomfortable moments (and a few joints of marijuana), the group begins to talk. Soon, the intimacy of the group grows intense. They have a taste of transparent, honest relationships. But they know that when they go back to school on Monday, there is a good chance things will return to normal. The best youth culture has to offer many youth relationally is fragmented experiences of intimacy that can seldom be sustained.

Characteristically, teenagers do not have the relational and developmental capacity to maintain a single, committed relationship for an extended period of time. They flow in and out of relationships with their peers. This year's enemy is next year's best friend. Even in more serious relationships, the skills that are learned the best are the skills of "dating," "going together" and "breaking up."

But one of the keys to successful adult relationships beyond the superficial level (for example, parenting, marriage and church membership) is a commitment to demonstrate love in spite of pain, conflict or frustration. Could it be that one of the reasons for the Western nations' devastating divorce rate is that our young people are not learning the skills of genuine love? Young people learn to love through the long haul as they are surrounded by adults who, over and over again, demonstrate this kind of enduring, long-suffering love.

I recently talked with a man whose wife decided that their marriage was "not going to work out." She was not interested in counseling. She just wanted their marriage to end. Her final words to him as he walked out the door sounded hauntingly reminiscent of the words a teenager would use to break up with her boyfriend: "I just want to be friends."

If a teenage boy stops feeling love for his girlfriend or he is attracted to another girl, he can simply break up and go out with someone else. In a marriage, when a man stops feeling love for his wife or is attracted to someone else's wife, the mature Christian adult behaves very differently.

In youth culture, the natural, God-ordained process of attraction—"falling in love"—has been elevated to consume a young person's understanding of what real love is. Teenagers have learned to believe that they are simply victims of a feeling that comes and goes. Consequently, they learn to obey "that loving feeling" at all costs. As a result, increasing numbers of our young people enter adulthood lacking the relational maturity to establish long-term relationships.

Cognitive Fragmentation

Because teenagers now have less time in dialogue with adults, the door has been opened for the media to play a much more powerful role in the formation of young people's values. Even the *TV Guide* has acknowledged that the more children are isolated from their parents, the more susceptible those children are to the power of the television:

> The children who are more inclined to go along with television, to lap up its messages uncritically, are those who have received little in the way of guidance at home, hence their susceptibility to whatever the big tube sends their way.[3]

What makes the television's impact so potent is the radical change that has taken place in the way we process information. Neil Postman, in his challenging book *Amusing Ourselves to Death*, claims that American society has actually gone through a transformation in the way we think, having moved from a word-centered culture to an image-centered culture. It is likely, Postman argues, that in their time most of the first fifteen U.S. presidents would not have even been recognized if the average American had passed them on the street. But by contrast, when we think of Richard Nixon, Billy Graham or Albert Einstein, what comes to our minds is an image, and most of us have few words to link with that image.

Postman points to the inherent danger of this new kind of thinking:

> You can only photograph a particular fragment of the here-and-now—a cliff or a certain terrain, in a certain condition of light; a wave at a moment in time, from a particular point of

view. And just as "nature" and "the sea" cannot be photo-
graphed, such larger abstractions as truth, honor, love, false-
hood cannot be talked about in the lexicon of pictures.[4]

Our culture's growing dependence on images for thinking has
limited our ability to make moral decisions or even understand
abstract moral concepts. When our young people are taught to
speak and think primarily in the language of images and not of
logical thoughts, moral principles and Christian values may
sound to them like so much babbling in a different language.
Living in an image-centered culture produces adults who are
moved more by impression than by rational thinking.

The ability to sustain a logical, linear argument is developed
primarily in the context of extended discourse with thinking
adults. Because of their isolation from the world of adults in our
educational system, teenagers seldom have opportunity to learn
and practice the skills of assessment and judgment with those
who actually *have* those skills. As a result, teenagers have learned
to argue anecdotally (and to respond most energetically to
anecdotal "proofs"), using fragmented images and emotional
stories instead of logical argument.

As a professor of history at Smith College, R. Jackson Wilson
has had twenty-five years to observe students and their abilities.
His observation of his current students' abilities confirms this
thesis: "Students are ready to tell you how they feel about an
issue, but they have never learned how to construct a rational
argument to defend their opinions."[5]

Teenagers' isolation from adults has left many of them unable
to think critically. They are easily swayed by what feels right at
the moment, whether it is going to church, buying a $200 pair
of tennis shoes or having sex. Without the habit of critical
thinking, our teenagers become easy prey to anyone who has
something to sell.

Moral Handicap

The haunting story of fourteen-year-old Rod Matthews serves as a warning to a culture gone adrift. Rod was not interested in the things that normally interest teenagers. Neither sports nor books were enough to quench his insatiable boredom. Only one thing excited him: death. He spent hours watching the video *Faces of Death,* a collection of film clips of people dying violently. Rod's curiosity about death led him to want to see death personally, not just on the television or movie screen.

Eventually, he found a way to satisfy his curiosity. One winter afternoon he lured a friend out into the woods and proceeded to beat him to death with a baseball bat. During his trial for murder, the most telling remark was made by a child psychiatrist who was asked to give a clinical evaluation of Rod's condition. The doctor's assessment was that Rod was not insane in the conventional sense but that he simply didn't "know right from wrong. . . . He [was] *morally handicapped"* (emphasis mine).[6]

Rod's story represents the extreme result of a society that has abandoned its responsibility for teaching moral values to its children. The horizontal peer culture is not enough. When the vertical structure connecting children with adults has eroded, should we be surprised that our children grow up having difficulty establishing any firm values of their own?

The "Just Say No" campaign was indicative of the moral (in)abilities of our young people. After spending millions of dollars on drug education campaigns that focused on giving young people rational reasons for not taking drugs, the U.S. government determined in the 1980s that a rational approach was not the way to reach this generation of young people. The "Just Say No" campaign was developed at least partly because leaders recognized that this new generation makes major moral decisions not by rational argument but by being "sold" a certain standard. (The "Just Say No" campaigns were essentially ineffective in the lower-income areas of inner cities. In these cases, the horizontal peer dependence, particularly in gangs, outweighed any message from the mainstream culture.)

The young people who are fortified with significant relationships with adults are consistently the ones who are able to resist involvement in negative behaviors. Their relationship with these adults gives teenagers perhaps the most compelling argument for making healthy moral choices. Stephen Glenn and Jane Nelsen's research confirms this thesis:

> Peer influence correlates closely with the rise in rebellion, resistance, chemical abuse, and promiscuity. Children who have strong perceptions of closeness and trust with significant adults are highly resistant to peer influence and are more heavily influenced by those adults who validate them for who they are.[7]

Young people in our culture are increasingly unprepared to live as mature adults. For the most part, they enter adulthood relationally retarded, cognitively fragmented and morally handicapped. Their own culture often keeps them trapped in this immaturity, training them to be reactive victims rather than proactive Christians.

The Hidden Hazards of Youth Culture

Perhaps the most tragic shift over the past fifty years has been that we have begun to treat adolescents as adults rather than as children in transition toward adulthood. Although there are many things about being a teenager that are to be honored and enjoyed, adolescence, like childhood, is a stage that one should outgrow. The result of successfully completing adolescence is to be no longer an adolescent, just as the goal of childhood is to be strong and mature enough to be no longer a child.

But for teenagers in our culture, the lines between childhood and adulthood have become increasingly blurred, so much so that many adults well into their twenties still behave in a way characteristic of adolescents. With few clear rites of passage, teenagers are in the double bind of being expected to make adult decisions in a world that persistently juvenilizes them.

When we idolize youth as an end in itself, we remove the healthy protection that growing things require. George Will pinpoints this problem: "In Randall Jarrell's novel *Pictures from an Institution* a foreign visitor says, 'You Americans do not rear children, you incite them; you give them food and shelter and applause.' The problem is juvenophilia."[8]

Cultures, by definition, pass on the best of what has been learned so that the best of that culture may be maintained. In other words, one of the prime functions of a culture is to perpetuate itself and its values. In the same way, the development of a separate youth culture has functioned to perpetuate adolescence.

The very existence of a youth culture places teenagers at cross-purposes with their own development. They need to leave the world of youth, but during their teenage years they are indoctrinated into a culture that functions to maintain their immaturity.

Street gangs provide the most blatant picture of the dysfunctional power of a youth culture. In a gang, there is authority, strict rules and punishment, and a shared sense of values. But all these norms are determined by a group of young people not yet mature enough to make wise decisions consistently. The first and often only solution to a problem is violence (exactly what we might expect if a preschool group was left to govern itself). We can expect that any system run by children or teenagers will be dysfunctional.

In our churches, if groups of more than ten young people are sitting together in worship, they tend to act, at best, like children. They snicker, rattle candy wrappers, and often simply get up and leave the balcony. But if the same youth are sitting with their parents or divided up among the total congregation, they, almost without exception, imitate the behavior of the adults they are with.

We recently completed a six-week confirmation class for a group of thirty sixth-graders. The boys in the class were so energetic that they came to be affectionately labeled the "Young Nazis." Even with two pastors and three older high-school youths in the group, the boys were successful in disrupting the class every week.

But on the day that the members of the class were introduced to the session by their "Elder Friends" (who sat next to them), we wondered if we were in a different class. The boys were quiet, attentive and respectful, imitating the values of the adults in the group.

Stephen Glenn has estimated that by the time an average American teenager is sixteen years old, he is "as morally mature as a 1950's 12-year-old, and five years behind European kids in abstract thinking."[9]

Youth culture, like most youth ministries, is essentially an orphaning structure. It does not carry its members through life; rather, it orphans them at the very time they are most in need of a stable culture. The isolation of teenagers from the world of adults has severely hindered the processes that lead teenagers to mature adulthood. The structures that carry young people to adulthood must become the focus of youth ministry for the next generation.

Implications for Ministry

1. The most important priority a church can have in its work with

teenagers is providing them with opportunities for significant dialogue and relationships with mature Christian adults. This priority does not require a massive budget or an extensive program. It does require a group of adult leaders in the church who will make the creation of relationships between adults and teenagers the central priority of the youth ministry.

2. Churches must not depend on the communication vehicles of youth culture (television with its frantic change of scenery for the chronically bored, "contemporary" music with its "make me feel good" priority, and successful athletes with their stories of freedom from failure) to carry the demanding claims of the gospel. All of these means may be helpful thresholds to the Christian life, but they are not sufficient to carry the responsibility for developing spiritual maturity.

3. We must not be afraid to instill the value of participating in weekly corporate worship with the entire church family as a central priority for the youth ministry.

Wild Hair—Challenge the youth and their leaders in the church to fast from the cultural vehicles of value transmission (television, recorded music, movies) for one month and share their experiences at the end of the month.

• • • • • • • • • • • • • • • • • •

I am convinced that the very foundations upon which we engage in Christian education are shaking. And while a host of builders attempt with varying degrees of success to shore them up, there is a dearth of architects engaged in designing new structures. The church's educational problem rests not in its educational program, but in the paradigm or model which undergirds its educational ministry—the agreed-upon frame of reference which guides its educational efforts.

JOHN WESTERHOFF, *Will Our Children Have Faith?*

I take a very low view of "climates of opinion." In his own subject every man knows that all discoveries are made and all errors corrected by those who ignore the "climate of opinion."

C. S. LEWIS, *The Problem of Pain*

Successful youth ministry in this era certainly doesn't require bigger and better programs; rather, kids are looking for simplicity and effectiveness. Instead of building a Rolls-Royce with all the amenities, we need to build a simple Jeep—rugged, durable, and flexible. Your most effective planning tool may be your eraser.

TIM SMITH, *Youthworker*

The day of the "broadcast" is over. "Narrowcasting" has become essential for radio and television to survive. The day of youth ministry "broadcasting" is over as well.

MARK SENTER, *The Coming Revolution in Youth Ministry*

When one part of [an] organism is treated in isolation from its interconnections with another, as though the problem were solely its own, fundamental change is not likely. The symptom is apt to recycle, in the same or different form, in the same or different member. Trying to "cure" a person in isolation from his or her family . . . is as misdirected, and ultimately ineffective, as transplanting a healthy organ into a body whose imbalanced chemistry will destroy the new one as it did the old. It is easy to forget that the same "family" of organs that rejects a transplant contributed to the originally diseased part becoming "foreign."

EDWIN FRIEDMAN, *Generation to Generation*

4
It Only
Makes Sense
The Vision
of Family-Based
Youth Ministry

When I came to First Presbyterian in Nashville seven years ago, I inherited a small but strong Sunday-night program—a core group of youth who came fairly regularly and who seemed to love being together. Most of this core group went to the same two schools. Actually, since one of these schools was only for boys and the other only for girls, students from these two schools moved in almost identical social circles.

I soon realized that despite the homogeneous nature of that active group, there were young people from twenty-one different schools on our church rolls. Naturally, my first plan was to try to expand the Sunday-night program so that it included teenagers from as many different schools as possible.

I worked with our volunteer leaders to come up with fun, exciting programs for each week. And after six months of diligent planning and work, the group had grown from about thirty to an average of almost thirty-two. Although different youth were coming, I had simply exchanged the "old guard" with a "new guard." The Sunday-night program seemed to be going nowhere.

With passion, I began trying new program after new program. But it seemed that each new program I tried basically hit the same ceiling. Whether we were only having fun or having more diligent Bible study or doing service projects or some combination of the three, the group would settle into a ho-hum pattern that seemed to be going nowhere.

As I tried to keep the Sunday-night program alive, I began to see the need for discipleship groups for young people who wanted something a little deeper than we could give in Sunday school or youth group. So we created "house groups," which met for a year. The young people involved in these groups had some great experiences building friendships with Christian adults, but all in all, the house group plan met with only limited success.

About the time I was thinking of creating yet another new program, God put Earl Palmer in my path. I don't remember what his message was about, but his comments about growth in the world of nature opened up a new way of thinking for me. He explained that by and large things grow by two means: either by being planted or by being pruned.

It had never crossed my mind that I could make my youth program grow by getting rid of something. I realized that what I really needed was not to come up with another creative program but to cut something. Since I had arrived in Nashville, I had created new program after new program, but I seldom got rid of any of the old ones. The multitude of programs were choking each other out. I was in a jungle. Something had to go.

I returned to Nashville with a new vision. Program-hacking machete in hand, I began to examine our ministry for some place to cut. The problem was that there was something good about everything we were doing. Youth group had an appeal to some; the house groups were definitely meeting a need. I could try to cut Sunday school, but only if I was interested in rapid relocation. Clearly, this was not going to be a choice of cutting something bad from the program. That task would have been easy. But I knew that our ministry was being choked out by too many "good things."

I was also beginning to recognize that our "plain old vanilla" youth group had hit an invisible ceiling. We were trying to reach such a broad spectrum of young people in that weekly meeting that for the majority it was not an effective doorway to involvement.[1]

Eventually, I settled on getting rid of the Sunday-night youth group (a sacred tradition of most Southern churches). More than any other of our programs, it simply wasn't going anywhere. And it was becoming increasingly difficult to have a program that would be meaningful for both the "Mother Teresas" and the "Al Capones" of our group.

At the same time, I was beginning to develop some preliminary ideas about a family-based youth ministry. My initial research confirmed over and over again that real power for faith formation was not in the youth program but in the families and the extended family of the church.

The idea of "nuking" our Sunday-night youth group was not immediately embraced by everyone in our congregation. A group of parents lobbied strongly for the status quo. My colleagues on the church staff kept giving me those "I'm-sorry-you're-going-to-the-gallows" looks. And the rumor began to be circulated around town that we had simply given up on our youth ministry because no one ever came.

But for two years, we actually did go without Sunday-night

"youth group" (and lived to tell about it). By the end of our second year, weekly attendance had increased to almost sixty teenagers. Since we now had only one weekly youth program (Sunday school), instead of three or four, we were able to increase significantly both the quality of our programming and the number of young people involved.

We used Sunday nights primarily for focused special events for the six classes. For example, one Sunday the tenth-graders would go to the soup kitchen; the next Sunday, the ninth-graders and their parents would ride go-karts. The structure allowed for flexibility in scheduling without the expectation that every student be involved every week. In addition, a few youth-initiated discipleship groups met every Sunday afternoon.

Of course, not everyone was pleased, and many were vocal about their concerns. During these two years, it seemed as if I spent every Youth Committee meeting defending our current program and arguing about whether or not we should "go back" to having traditional youth group.

By the middle of the second year, I began to realize a tremendous (unexpected) byproduct of our minimal programming: I now had a huge group of parents more eager to be involved than ever. Without knowing quite how I had gotten there, I was now exactly where I wanted to be—with a group of enthusiastic parents willing to invest in our youth ministry.

As 1992 began, I started to meet weekly with an incredible group of eight parents who went to work with a passion to create a broad-based vision for our youth ministry. After 200 hours of work, the group made an extensive, thirty-page recommendation that provided for significant involvement by both the parents and the teenagers in the ongoing planning process for our ministry. They designed a flexible program that did not lock us into any one activity for too long.

The heart of our story is not what our program looks like now, because I am sure that by the time this book goes to print, we will have changed the format again. The answer is not to be found in any one structure but in the process of creating the structure.

The Twofold Strategy
When I left the church in Texas where I had served in youth ministry for six years, the teenagers and their parents decided to have a celebration roast for my wife, Susan, and me. As is expected at such an event, people spoke warmly from their vast store of selective memories about the "success" of our youth ministry. I remember that writing my final article for the church newsletter helped me focus more clearly on what success in youth ministry really looks like.

In that article, I explained that we really wouldn't know how successful our program had been for ten years or so. Would these young people still be growing in Christ? Would they have chosen to be proactive Christians, taking the initiative in knowing and serving God? I knew that all of our exciting programs would be like mist in the wind unless we had given our teens something that lasts.

It is now ten years since I left Waco. Almost without exception, those young people who are growing in their faith as adults were teenagers who fit into one of two categories: either (1) they came from families where Christian growth was modeled in at least one of their parents, or (2) they had developed such significant connections with adults within the church that it had become an extended family for them.[2] *How often they attended youth events (including Sunday school and discipleship groups) was not a good predictor of which teens would and which would not grow toward Christian adulthood.*

When a church makes the first priority of its youth ministry attracting teens, those churches will choose almost exclusively young, single, enthusiastic, good-looking adults as youth workers. Typically, that strategy works beautifully in the short run. But I agree with Ben Patterson when he argues that young Christians need more:

> A twenty-year-old youth worker may be effective in getting the kids' attention, but he or she often isn't able to bridge the gap between kids and the adult community, primarily because the youth worker isn't yet a full member of that adult community. That's not the youth worker's fault; it is, however, a serious limitation.[3]

The beginning of a family-based youth ministry involves a shift in perception. Our goal is no longer simply to have a "strong youth program" (that is, have many teens active in many activities). When, for example, having a Sunday-night youth group was not helping our teenagers move toward mature Christian adulthood, our church chose to get rid of that regular event—even if it meant weakening the "youth program."

A startling study done by the United Church of Australia documented the long-term impact of dividing the church into age-specific groups. The researchers discovered that people who grew up in church attending worship and not Sunday school were much more likely to be involved in church as adults than were those young people who had attended only Sunday school without attending worship.[4]

The results of this study clearly call into question our myopic focus on creating a successful youth ministry. If this conclusion is transferable to Christians of other nations (and I know of no reason why it would not be), there is no such thing as successful youth ministry that isolates teenagers from the community of faith.

Priority Number One: Empower Parents

Our isolated youth programs cannot compete with the formative power of the family. Over and over again, I have seen the pattern. Young people may pull away from their parents' influence during their teenage years, but as a general rule, as adults, they return to the tracks that were laid by their parents. I picture it like the diagram in figure 2, where the influence of the nuclear family is like the walls of a canal.

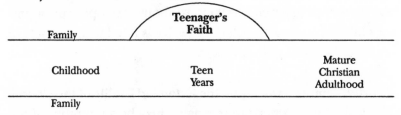

Figure 2. The Family as a Primary Faith Nurturing Structure

I pulled away from my parents during my teenage years by becoming "more spiritual" than they. I was sure that because I carried my Bible more often than they did, I took it more seriously than my Presbyterian minister father and my missionary mother. During my college years especially, I stretched as far as I could to get away from the traditional Christianity they practiced.

But now, as a minister in the same denomination as my father, in a church very similar in style to those he served, I recognize that much of my pulling away was only temporary. And although there are a few significant differences (created through my connections with an extended Christian family), for the most part I have returned to the core Christian values of my family.

Like a rubber band, young people may stretch away from their parents' values during their teenage years. But when they become adults, they will ordinarily return to the core values of their parents.

These parents need help in learning how to provide for the Christian nurture of their children. But youth workers must not merely do for the youth what their Christian parents cannot, or will not, do for them. Instead, we must endeavor to equip those parents to communicate the faith to their teenagers themselves.[5]

Equipping parents for their work as the primary nurturers of their children's faith has been an essentially untapped resource in youth ministry.[6] Churches can learn to be just as intentional about equipping parents as they are about developing programs for children and youth. Chapter twelve is filled with a variety of ideas for beginning this process.

Priority Number Two: Equip the Extended Family of the Church
The isolation of American teenagers may be a symptom of the rootlessness of the American family. Many parents, in a desire to build security for their children, have chosen to isolate their family into a world of its own, a world in which "family comes first."

But this "my family first" attitude, especially among Christians, has, in fact, only served to sever nuclear families from the very structures that can give their children lasting values and clear identity. Without strong ties to specific extended families (for example, church, neighborhood, nation), nuclear families have become self-perpetuating breeding grounds for rootlessness and alienation.

Jesus redefined the nature of the family for the Christian, placing a high priority on the extended family of brothers and sisters in Christ. When he was told that his mother and his brothers were outside looking for him, he could have said, "My family comes first." Instead he responded, "Who are my mother and my brothers?" He looked around at the people sitting with him and said, "Here are my mother and my brothers! Whoever does God's will is my brother and sister and mother" (Mk 3:31-35).

In even more radical terms, Jesus challenged his listeners to resist the natural temptation to place family loyalty on a par with loyalty to God: "Whoever comes to me and does not hate father and mother, wife and children, brothers and sisters, yes, and even life itself, cannot be my disciple" (Lk 14:26 NRSV).

Of course, Jesus was not advocating a wholesale rejection of the nuclear family. His concern is that those who follow him understand clearly the nature of their "first family." The unswerving, ultimate priority of the Christian is the glory of God and his kingdom. Sometimes the nuclear family will support these priorities and other times not. The standard by which the nuclear family is to be judged is by the new family of brothers and sisters in Christ.

In his book *The First Urban Christians,* Wayne Meeks points out that one of the most stinging critiques the ancient Romans made about Christianity was that it destroyed the family. There was no more cherished value in Roman society than the family. Every Roman institution depended on it.[7] The Romans rightly understood the Christian faith as a threat to the family, because Christianity advocated the subordination of family loyalty to one's loyalty to the new Christian family.

So the second priority of family-based youth ministry must be to provide a new "first family" for our teenagers by allowing them to experience the extended family of the church (not to be confused with an extended family of teenagers in the church).

But what about young people who do not come from Christian homes? In many ways, family-based youth ministry has particular benefits for those whose parents are outside the church. Youth who come from non-Christian homes especially need a circle of adult Christians to model the Christian life for them. These teenagers need more than their youth leaders, they (even more than young people from Christian homes) need the secure lifelong structure that a connection to the entire church provides.[8]

A retired Air Force pilot reminiscing to young people about his fearful and faith-demanding flights in World War II may seem like just an old man telling stories. But those stories can be the gospel made real, good news "with skin on it." As youth hear adults speaking of their own faith experiences, they begin to learn how to describe their own experience of God.

There are many ways for adults to be with teenagers without being their teachers. One of the churches I described in chapter one was accomplishing this goal quite successfully without even knowing it. That Texas pastor lamented that his church had virtually "no youth program." But in his small church, 15 out of 18 young people were active in some program of the church *weekly*—ushering, singing in the "adult" choir, helping in the nursery or teaching children's Sunday school. This church had, without even planning to do so, created multiple opportunities for its young people to be influenced by Christian adults in the church. If this church is ever able to create a "successful youth program," its may destroy its youth ministry.

Three Models for Youth Ministry

In struggling to determine what to do about our ministry to teenagers, I discovered that most churches are frustrated with their youth programs. Not only are church leaders not getting what they want, but those same leaders can't seem to agree on exactly what they do want.

As I looked for churches who were doing youth ministry effectively, I discovered a distinct pattern. Every church I looked at was using one of three distinct models. I have not seen a youth program yet that does not fit into one of these three categories. The principles of family-based youth ministry can be implemented in any of the three models. Either of the first two can be quite effective. The third is the model used by the majority of churches and almost always results in a sense of frustration and failure.

Fortune 500

I call the first model the "Fortune 500" youth ministry. In a Fortune 500 program, the congregation and the church expect excellence in everything—great communication, great pastoral care, great student leadership development, great missions, great education, great volunteer recruitment and training, great youth music program, excellence in everything. The favorite phrase heard around a Fortune 500 youth ministry is "We can do it better."

This model of ministry has many advantages. It tends to produce a high-quality, visible program with many teenagers involved and very creative programming. The church becomes known around the community as a church that makes youth ministry a real priority.

One disadvantage of this kind of program is that the high level of programming can inadvertently train the youth of the church to be good consumers, to demand superior programming before pursuing their faith as adults. The other disadvantage is that this type of program is fairly expensive. According to my rough estimates based on general research of churches with this style program, a church can expect to pay between $1,500 and $2,000 annually *for each student* active in the program on a weekly basis. In other words, if a church wants a "Fortune 500" program with 100 teens involved weekly, it will cost the church between $150,000 and $200,000 annually (with the majority of the budget typically going to staffing).

A typical Fortune 500 youth ministry has a large full-time youth ministry staff (usually between three and eight full-time workers). Some of these churches have extensive intern programs with scores of paid workers investing in the youth of the church.

Stick to Your Knitting

I call the second model of youth ministry "Stick to Your Knitting." This type of program revolves around a single element of the youth ministry. It could be the youth choir, the mission program, Bible study, evangelism, Sunday school. The church simply chooses (intentionally or accidentally) what it will focus on with its teenagers and strives to do that one thing very well. Around a church that has a Stick to Your Knitting style of youth ministry, the favorite phrase is "We may not do everything, but we sure have a great . . ."

The advantage of this kind of program is that it can be much less expensive than the Fortune 500 model, while involving just as many young people. Teens are likely to feel involved on a deeper level if they are invested in a single program rather than dabbling in a variety of events.

The single disadvantage to the Stick to Your Knitting model is that it lacks the balance teenagers need as they are developing a clear understanding of the Christian life. Young people can come to equate the whole of the Christian life with a single focus. For example, a church whose "knitting" is the youth choir may find that for some young people the choir makes up their entire faith identity. Or a church that makes missions a primary emphasis may neglect worship or Christian education or discipleship.

The Fellowship of Christian Athletes and Youth With A Mission are two ministries that have developed this model of youth ministry well. Both of these groups have a single focus and have emerged from the youth ministry confusion of the 1980s with a consistently growing ministry to teenagers.[9]

Comparative Confusion
No model can provide everything, and any model a church chooses will have disadvantages. But while either of the first two models will work effectively if either strategy is embraced fully, most churches, in an unrealistic effort to avoid all the disadvantages, opt for a youth ministry with no clear vision at all. They then almost inevitably fall into the model I call "Comparative Confusion," the worst of all possible choices.

The church with a Comparative Confusion youth ministry places great demands on its youth program. These demands are not based on what is realistic for that church considering its budget. Rather, the expectations are based on the fact that "not enough teenagers are involved in our church," while other churches seem to be reaching young people much more successfully.

The favorite question of the Comparative Confusion church is, "Why can't we just do what they're doing at that other church?" Since the focus is not set, this style of program has the apparent advantage of flexibility and the potential for constant change. But leaders in Comparative Confusion youth ministries have difficulty acknowledging or enjoying their own accomplishments as long as another church seems to be doing more.

The obvious disadvantage is that this model produces a perpetual attitude of frustration and failure. When the identity of a program is based solely on how it compares with other churches, frustration almost always results. Does the church across town have a great youth choir? The Comparative Confusion church will work like crazy to "stay competitive." Whether it's concerts, small groups, missions or the latest youth ministry fad, the

Comparative Confusion youth ministry remains in a reactive posture, responding to the loudest voices or the priorities of the newest staff or volunteers. This model prevents churches from ever sticking with any one priority long enough to let it work. Because of the constant sense of failure that is a part of this style of ministry, the Comparative Confusion church can expect a rapid turnover of youth workers.

Family-based youth ministry works best with either of the first two models. A "Fortune 500" youth ministry needs the undergirding that comes from involving families and the extended family of the church. A "Stick to Your Knitting" youth ministry would be wise to approach its single priority in ministry from a family-based perspective. The key is that a church become intentional about choosing its model for youth ministry and then undergird that model with family-based programming.

The Foundational Focus

Jesus ends his "Sermon on the Mount" (Mt 7:24-27) with a marvelous parable about two houses. From what Jesus tells us, we can assume that the houses were structurally very similar. Nothing about the buildings themselves determined their destiny. But one of them crashed under the weight of the wind and the other withstood the storm. Only one thing made the difference: the foundation.

Family-based youth ministry is not a "new wing" to be added to a church's youth ministry "house." It is not an optional enrichment program. Family-based youth ministry is a foundational model.

Much that has been done in traditional youth ministry over the past fifty years has been highly effective. In other words, the houses have been well designed. But because the foundation has often been limited, so has the long-term impact.

What family-based youth ministry has to offer is less a blueprint than a vision for youth ministry that lasts for the long haul. Like Jesus in the parable, I am advocating a different foundation, not a different floor plan.

Colossians 1:28-29 expresses the goal of family-based youth ministry:

> We proclaim him, admonishing and teaching everyone with all wisdom, so that we may present everyone perfect in Christ. To this end I labor, struggling with all his energy, which so powerfully works in me.

The first principle of family-based youth ministry is this primary goal: to equip young people to grow toward mature Christian adulthood (that is, to present them "perfect" or "complete in Christ").

Making this goal our first priority over the short-term objective of getting students to come to our meetings may radically transform our attitudes about youth ministry. Instead of trying harder and harder to make the old "tried and true" programs work, we can be open to a myriad of new possibilities that can lead us more directly to our primary goal.

Steven Covey tells a wonderful story that provides us with a picture of how easy it is to confuse our short-term objectives with our long-term goals. Covey invites us to imagine a man going to the eye doctor for the very first time. The man explains how much trouble he is having seeing things; everything is blurry.

After a cursory look into the patient's eyes, the doctor takes off his own glasses, gives them to his patient and says, "Here, try these." The patient puts the glasses on, takes a moment for his eyes to adjust to the new lenses and quickly realizes he cannot see a thing. He responds, "It's worse now than before!"

The doctor answers in an obvious tone of frustration, "Hey,

they've worked great for me for ten years. Just try a little harder and I'm sure they'll work."

Simply trying harder and harder at the same old things we've done in youth ministry over the past few decades will not address the foundational crisis in youth ministry. But family-based youth ministry offers a structure in which each church can develop its own prescription.

The prescription of family-based youth ministry creates a foundation for whatever model a church chooses to use to reach its teenagers, recognizing that no one programming strategy will work effectively over the long haul. By focusing on equipping parents and the extended Christian family, churches can maintain an open and flexible stance toward the changes that will be demanded of youth ministry in the twenty-first century.

Implications for Ministry

1. Before a church begins the process of planning programs for its teenagers, its leadership needs to be intentional about building a foundation for the youth ministry. Equipping parents and the extended family of adults in the church to provide ongoing nurture for the church's youth must be the first priority.

2. As a church begins to develop its youth program, its leadership would be wise to decide early on their model for youth ministry and budget accordingly. As an obvious example, if the church wants a long-lasting ministry to hundreds of youth, they should not budget for a part-time college student to run the program.

3. If the church decides not to have a "Fortune 500" style of youth ministry, they should focus in a single area—for example, music, missions, discipleship or families. The leadership should be prepared to support this focused program when criticisms come.

4. There are basically two types of family-based programs—those to equip parents to effectively nurture their children in the Christian faith (for example, classes and events for parents) and those that give teenagers the opportunity to be with adults (such as classes and events for parents and teenagers together).

Wild Hair—Take a break from the regular youth program (for a year or more) to get the church's attention fixed on the priority of establishing a long-term plan for youth ministry.

It is common wisdom to suggest that churches lose a great many of their youth to non-affiliation during their college years. Studies have shown, however, that the greatest share of disaffiliation among youth occurs "before college, and it is related to how important religion is to the parents [and] the amount of love and affection given a child (i.e., more love associated with a greater tendency to affiliate)."

MILTON COALTER, quoted in *The Presbyterian (U.S.A.) General Assembly Report of the Task Force on Membership*

The paradox, therefore, is that genuine autonomy—understood as mature independence rather than simply isolation from others—is best achieved within the context of a well-functioning family, not in its absence.

EDWARD ZIGLAR and **ELIZABETH GILMAN,** in *Rebuilding the Nest*

It is no coincidence that all twentieth-century totalitarian orders labored to destroy the family as a locus of identity and meaning apart from the state. Totalitarianism strives . . . to require that individuals never allow their commitments to specific others—family, friends, comrades—to weaken their commitment to the state. To this idea, which can only be described as evil, the family stands in defiance.

JEAN BETHKE ELSHTAIN, in *Rebuilding the Nest*

While you wait for your teenagers to grow up, you can take comfort in the fact that by the time young people reach their mid-twenties, their lines are almost always identical to the lines their parents drew. Even those who do not like certain attributes of their parents find themselves following their parents' patterns. So perhaps the point is not how we can get our kids to behave as we want them to, but how can we be the kind of parents we ought to be so that when our kids are like us, we'll like what they are.

JAY KESLER, *Energizing Your Teenager's Faith*

5
Sitting on a
Gold Mine
The Power of the
Nuclear Family

I *loved talking to Jay. It seemed as if every time we talked, he would* have something positive to say about my work as his youth director ten years ago. Jay, now nearing thirty, with a family of his own, was involved in our program through junior high and high school. He even went on to join the youth ministry staff of the church. If anyone has, Jay has grown into a proactive Christian adult.

Not long ago, I decided to check out my family-based youth ministry theory with Jay. So I asked him, "How would you compare the impact your youth directors had on your Christian life with the impact your parents had?"

He said, "You guys were great, but honestly, I think if you had never been around, I would still be in the same place spiritually that I am today. My parents had a huge impact on my relationship with Christ."

It's time for a reality check. Youth ministries, in and of themselves, have limited power to produce lasting change in young people's lives.

The Hidden Curriculum of the Family

In the movie *Karate Kid,* Mr. Miagi, the wise old mentor, takes on the task of teaching karate to Daniel, an impatient young teenager who has asked for help. Daniel is eager to become an expert in martial arts as quickly as possible. But Mr. Miagi has other plans.

Instead of teaching his student karate moves, the master teacher begins rather unconventionally. The old man gives Daniel laborious tasks to accomplish, tasks which take days to complete—"paint de fence," "wax de car," "sand de floor." Naturally, Daniel, who simply wants to learn karate, becomes frustrated. After several weeks, all he has to show for his work is sore muscles and wasted hours (except for a great-looking fence, a shiny car and a very smooth floor). But Daniel still hasn't learned a bit of karate (or so he thinks).

What he doesn't realize (until Mr. Miagi takes a surprising swing at him) is that the mundane, repetitive and painful work has trained his muscles to move instinctively. Without knowing it, he has learned more karate than any set of lessons could teach. Beneath the apparently unrelated activity, the master teacher has a hidden curriculum.

Parents have this sort of formative effect on their children. All the youth group and Sunday-school lessons on "Communication," "Getting Along with Your Parents" and even "Discipleship" have minuscule impact compared to what children learn on a day-to-day basis as they "paint de fence" in their families.

I developed most of my emotional, relational and spiritual reflexes in my family. And despite all I have read and taught about parenting and communication, I, like most adults, find myself doing the very things my parents did, even though I promised myself I would never do them. Without a single "lesson" from my parents on adulthood, my muscles were trained.

I have an adolescent psychiatrist friend whose brain I pick as often as I get the chance. One day, I asked him to tell me in general what he does with teenagers he counsels. I'il never forget his response. "I always start with the family," he said. "If a child is coming to see a psychiatrist, it's usually not just the child who has the problem."

The point of this chapter is not whether parents *ought* to have such a formative effect on their children (though I do believe that the tremendous power of parents' influence on their children is part of God's design). But just as gravity pulls objects toward the ground, whether we want it to or not, so families have unparalleled influence on the development of their children's lives and character.

Many are under the illusion that peers have as much influence in teenagers' lives as their parents do. With the increasing isolation of youth from the world of adults, peer influence may indeed be significant, but such influence is almost always short-lived. I like Kevin Huggins's description of the limited power that peers have in influencing long-term values:

> Although peers sometimes do exercise more control over an adolescent's choice of dress, music, entertainment, etc., only when parents are extremely negligent do peers exercise more control over the teen's choice of beliefs and relational styles than [the parents] do. In the vast majority of cases parents remain the single most important influence in the development of an adolescent's personality.[1]

In my work, I get to do quite a bit of premarital counseling. As a general rule, I spend a great deal of time with each couple talking about each of their parents—how they argued, how each partner is like or unlike his or her parents, and so on. I *always* ask about the parents. But in eight years of doing this kind of counseling, I have never found it relevant to ask about their best friends (or even about their youth minister!).

Because of the extensive exposure parents have to their own children,[2] they leave an indelible impression that radically affects how receptive their children will be to the gospel. There is overwhelming evidence that parents are, almost always, the single most significant determining factor in the development of their children.

For Better . . .

Research has repeatedly shown the strong correlation between healthy family ties and positive social behavior in teenagers. Merton and Irene Strommen, in their broad-based adolescent-parent study which surveyed 8,156 young people and 10,467 parents, confirmed this connection. They discovered that the strength of the relationship between parents and their teenagers fortifies teenagers with the courage to make wise choices. The study discovered that teenagers from close families were the least likely to be involved in high-risk behavior.[3]

Another study showed a strong correlation between the amount of time parents spent with their teenage children and the teenagers' ability to resist sexual pressure. Sixty-one percent of those young people who described their parents as "seldom or never" spending time with them had experienced sexual contact, compared to only 39 percent of those whose parents frequently committed time to them.[4]

Parents' influence extends even beyond personality and moral development to the world of academics. The National Merit Scholars organization recently completed a study in which they sought to identify the factors that influence these teenagers' high achievement. The research indicated that all these students have one subtle and somewhat surprising factor in common: they eat dinner with their families almost every day.[5]

Laurence Steinberg, professor of child and family studies at the University of Wisconsin, completed an extensive study on academic performance. He found, not surprisingly, that parents who developed close ties to the schools were the parents of children with the strongest academic records.[6]

Building a level of family closeness that fortifies children and youth is much less complicated than we might expect. Glenn and Nelsen estimate that building a structured ritual or activity into a family may take as little as thirty minutes a month with older children. Evidence indicates that those families that have built some traditional times to be together have children who experience much less difficulty than children who come from similar families but spend no intentional time together.[7]

... Or for Worse

I grew up watching Herman, Lily, Grandpa and Little Eddie on the seventies sit-com *The Munsters*. Herman was a tall, Frankenstein-esque character with green skin and railroad spikes protruding from his neck. Everyone in this family looked as if they had just stepped out of a horror movie. Everyone, that is, except one.

Little Eddie had an older sister (or was it a cousin?) who, by our society's standards, was beautiful: blond, vivacious, attractive in every way. But this young adult, whose name most of us have trouble remembering, *felt* inferior. Her family talked about her in whispering, sympathetic tones, silently embarrassed by her "disabilities." Her primary negative image of herself did not come from her friends or her work or society in general, but from her family.

In God's eyes, all the teenagers we work with are valuable and gifted. But if their family discounts those gifts, those young people may have difficulty believing us when we acknowledge them. Power is always a two-sided coin. Parents' power to build up is matched by their power to cause harm. And the evidence is equally convincing on both sides of the coin. Armand Nicholi captures the essence of the double-edged sword of parental power:

> If one factor influences the character development and emotional stability of a person, it is the quality of the relationship he experiences as a child with both of his parents. Conversely, if people suffering from severe non-organic emotional illness have one experience in common, it is the absence of a parent through death, divorce, a time-demanding job or absence for other reasons.[8]

In 1987, a study of violent rapists revealed that 60 percent of them were from single-parent homes. And a Michigan state study of teenagers who had committed homicides found that 75 percent of them were from broken homes.[9]

Bob Laurent, in his study of why teenagers feel alienated from the church, found a strong connection between problems at home and adolescents who felt acutely alienated from the church. He found that those who showed an across-the-board alienation from religion responded as follows to these statements:

"There are many conflicts and arguments in our family"—agree.

"In our family we respect each other's privacy"—disagree.

"Our family members are critical of each other"—agree.

"We do not forgive each other easily in our family"—agree.

"The members of our family hardly ever hurt each other's feelings"—disagree.[10]

For these young people, alienation from religion had little to do with church programming. These youth were alienated despite the quality of their churches' youth ministries. The conclusive factor for them was their family of origin.

The Laboratory of the Soul

In my childhood, my faith was formed as much around the dinner table as it was in the pew. Although my father is a pastor and my mother was a missionary, I don't remember hearing my parents talk much about God or about their own faith. What I do remember is our family meal.

Sometimes we would sing, sometimes pray a psalm, other times my dad would assign my brother or me to say "God is great." For me, it was in this seemingly minimal mealtime ritual, perhaps more than any other place, that my parents passed on the baton of their own faith.

As Christmas approached, we had a daily yule log with candles that we lit as a family in the evenings. And during Lent, my brother and I watched with pride as the cardboard One Great Hour of Sharing bank became heavier and heavier with our nickels and pennies. Along the way, with family prayer, spiritual traditions and weekly offering envelopes, my parents taught me that following Christ was a priority.

From ancient times, the family has always been the central faith-nurturing structure. As Edward Hayes points out,

> The first altar around which primitive people worshipped was the hearth, whose open fire burned in the center of the home. The next altar shrine was the family table, where meals were celebrated and great events in the personal history of the family were remembered. The priests and priestesses of these first rituals were the fathers and mothers of families.[11]

The teenagers in my church may be impressed by my stirring

message on "be quick to listen, slow to speak and slow to become angry" (Jas 1:19), but my wife and children are the ones who see if I really believe what I say. In the crucible of the family, pious masks evaporate before the fire of human frailty. In our families, our grand theologies boil down to how we live amid the frustrations of our most intimate relationships. Parents do not need to give lectures to their children in order for those children to learn what their parents believe. Their children will know soon enough. And children almost always "catch" the beliefs of their parents.

Some have described the family as the "laboratory for soul work."[12] And study after study has proven the accuracy of this title.[13] In 1986, Roger and Margaret Dudley from Andrews University studied the transmission of religious values from parents to their teenage children in the Seventh-day Adventist Church. Their conclusion? Even though the teenagers as a whole were slightly less traditional than their parents, the teenagers' values did, in fact, parallel the values of their parents. The study concluded, "Youth tend . . . to resemble their parents in religious values held . . . and even the independence of adolescence cannot usually obliterate these values completely."[14]

The Search Institute's 1990 National Study of Protestant Congregations indicated that the most important factor in a teenager's faith maturity was the level of "family religiousness." The particular family experiences most tied to greater faith maturity were the frequency with which an adolescent talked with mother and father about faith, the frequency of family devotions and the frequency with which parents and children together were involved in efforts, formal or informal, to help other people.[15]

As might be expected, the Search study's first recommendation for change in Christian education was to "equip mothers and fathers to play a more active role in the religious education of their children, by means of conversation, family devotions and family helping projects."[16]

Over 200 years ago, Jonathan Edwards made this same recommendation:

> Every Christian family ought to be as it were a little church consecrated to Christ, and wholly influenced and governed by his rule. And family education and order are some of the chief means of grace. *If these fail, all other means are likely to prove ineffectual.* If these are duly maintained, all the means of grace will be likely to prosper and be successful.[17] (emphasis mine)

Christian families provide one of the two most effective lifelong nurturing structures to carry young people to mature Christian adulthood.

Sitting on a Gold Mine

Traditionally, youth ministers have seen parents as an interruption, as obstacles to success in ministry. There's Darin's mom who corners us for "just a minute" to launch into a thirty-minute advertisement for the latest Christian book or tape. There's Gerald's dad who won't let Gerald come to youth group because it's "too silly." And there's Jennifer's mom who wishes youth group could be more fun, and she does the youth minister the favor of calling fifteen other parents to get their "objective feedback."

In many ways, a youth pastor's job would be much easier if he or she didn't have to deal with parents. But doing youth ministry without parents is like driving a car without the engine. From the top of a hill, this kind of car can coast at high speeds. But only for a while. Eventually it will stop. A car without an engine simply has no lasting power.

Most long-term youth ministers have resigned themselves to working like Sisyphus, the greedy king in Greek mythology, doomed to push a huge rock up a mountain only to watch it roll down again and to repeat the cycle over and over again throughout eternity.

But is the roller-coaster syndrome of youth ministry really necessary?

Jed Clampett and his *Beverly Hillbillies* family owned millions of dollars in oil wells for years as they struggled to stay alive in their mountain shack. They were sitting on a gold mine and didn't even know it.

Traditional youth ministers work themselves to the bone to hold their ministries together "with Scotch tape and paper clips," while at the same time ignoring the most powerful resource they have—teenagers' parents. Youth ministers and churches can no longer continue to view parents as neutral factors in their ministry to teenagers. Parents, simply by the way they raise their children, will either empower our ministries or sabotage them. Parents play a role second only to that of the Holy Spirit in building the spiritual foundation of their children's lives.

Implications for Ministry

1. Programming for parents of children and teenagers should be understood by the leadership of any church as central and foundational for the youth ministry. Christian education and youth committees can be just as intentional about this kind of programming as they are about the recruitment of Sunday-school teachers or the search for the right youth "program."

2. Intentional family-based programming does not need to replace age-specific youth programming. But unless family-based programming is given a higher priority than traditional youth programming, it is likely that the church will never get around to the task of building a solid foundation for its youth ministry.

3. Youth ministers can orient parents to the youth program each year by documenting for them the incredible power that they have in their children's lives and asking them to join the church as covenant partners in the Christian nurture of their children.

Wild Hair—Make it a priority of the youth ministry that all of the parents receive a personal visit from some representative of the church each year to strategize together about the Christian nurture of their son or daughter.

• • • • • • • • • • • • • • • • • •

To me it seems clear that our society is seriously malfunctioning in its role of preparing children for adulthood. The upheaval and disarray we are seeing in childrearing patterns are unprecedented in modern times.

VANCE PACKARD, *Our Endangered Children*

America's families, and their children, are in trouble, trouble so deep and pervasive as to threaten the future of our nation. The source of trouble is nothing less than a national neglect of children by those primarily engaged in their care—America's parents.

The 1970 White House Conference on the Family

My kid's all screwed up from heavy metal music and exposure to sexual videos at an early age. Don't blame me for his problems . . . I'm never home!

A PARENT, quoted in Bob DeMoss, *Learn to Discern*

The dreariness of the family's spiritual landscape passes belief.

ALLAN BLOOM, *The Closing of the American Mind*

My husband and I are either going to buy a dog or have a child. We can't decide whether to ruin our carpets or our lives.

RITA RUDNER, *Chicago Tribune Magazine*

6
The Critical Care Unit
The Peculiar Crisis in Today's Christian Family

O*ur fixer-upper," we called it, as we signed on the dotted line to* buy our first home. We were sure that all this house needed was just a little TLC. We could easily finish out a room here, build a fence there, add a little paint, a little wallpaper, and we'd have the house like we wanted it in no time.

Armed with the limited construction skills I had gained on youth mission trips, I took a week of vacation to build a fence around the backyard. I threw myself into the project with abandon. By the end of the first day, I had made three trips to Home Depot, read through the handy "How to Build Your Own Fence" instruction book, and begun measuring and putting stakes in the ground for the fenceposts. With so little tutoring or experience, I impressed myself with how easily I had picked up the finer points of carpentry. I was already putting together my mental list of the home improvement projects I would begin with the vacation time I had left over.

But after I was forced to battle a mid-March snowstorm and several days of freezing rain, my plans took a different turn. I came to the last day of my "vacation" far from finished with the fence. I went back to the drawing board and established the more realistic goal of simply getting all the fenceposts in place by the end of the day. By noon, I had begun digging the final posthole. But before I could finish congratulating myself, I hit rock. I had run into plenty of rocks in this process already. I knew exactly what to do. I would dig around it, find the edges and pull it out. Simple process. Or so I thought.

Three hours later, with my sledgehammer and pickax at my side, I was looking down at a hole six feet wide and a foot and a half deep. And I still hadn't found the edge of the rock. I did then what I should have done two hours and forty-five minutes earlier. I left the rock where it was and moved the hole.

There comes a time when we have to give up moving an obstacle and adjust our plan to the landscape we are given to work with. For most of my ministry with teenagers, I have been trying to move the "rock" of parents' failing to give attention to the spiritual growth of their children. For years I would whine, "If parents would just do their job, my work would be done."

I have given guilt-laden lectures to parents about their failures, comforting myself by blaming the parents for the natural frustrations of youth ministry. But simple solutions are usually no solution at all. My pushing parents to work harder was not the silver bullet for youth ministry that I thought it was. The more I dug around, the more I saw how deep the problem really was.

The simple solution of involving more parents in youth ministry is not enough. Parents do have incomparable power in the faith formation of their children, and we are foolish not to access this power in our youth ministries. But we live in an age of intense pressure on the family, and this pressure has produced a new pattern for parenting teenagers that severely hinders many Christian parents from impacting their children's faith. Any model that attempts to base itself on families must take seriously three factors affecting today's parents.

The Immature Christian Parent

When I first began applying the principles of family-based youth ministry, I held to the single strategy of letting parents take responsibility for the Christian nurture of their children. It wasn't long, though, before I realized that this simplistic focus only created frustration both for me and for the parents. The first obstacle I had to face in youth ministry was that most of the parents of the teenagers I was working with were not mature Christian adults themselves.

According to the 1990 Search Institute report, only *15 percent* of men between the ages of forty and fifty-nine have a mature, integrated faith.[1] Stated another way, it is likely that *85 percent* of our young people come from homes without a father to set an example of faithful discipleship. Is it any wonder, then, that 83 percent of ninth- and tenth-grade boys have an undeveloped faith?[2]

The same Search Institute report indicated that over half of sixteen- to eighteen-year-olds rarely or never have had family devotions, family projects to help others, or even talks with their fathers or other relatives about faith or God.[3] The report went on to document huge deficits among the Christian adult population of our churches: Sixty-one percent of adult church members *do not* give significant time or money to help others. Sixty-six percent of adult church members *do not* devote time to reading or studying the Bible. Seventy-two percent of adult church members *are not* involved in Christian education.[4]

The roots of the crisis in youth ministry, therefore, reach far beyond a simple analysis of the attendance patterns of our youth. If youth attendance is all we are interested in, we will scarcely even notice a problem. But attendance does not necessarily produce faith maturity.

In our church of over 3,000, we have about 200 teenagers on our rolls. On any given Sunday, the parents of 155 of those youth are not in worship.

One church's adult Sunday-school class took several months to allow each member to talk about their profession and how their faith relates to their profession. The idea was for the doctor to teach about being a Christian doctor and for the lawyer to teach about being a Christian lawyer—a different Christian professional each week. What became immediately obvious is that all of the professionals understood their profession quite deeply. They spoke in animated ways about their work and its challenges. But as it came time for them to speak about their faith, most spoke nervously and resorted to the kinds of clichés they had learned in children's Sunday school. For most, although they had continued growing and learning in their vocation, their spiritual development had stagnated.

Our youth ministries, for the most part, are no longer undergirded by mature Christian parents. And unless we pay attention to the significant spiritual deficits in our teenagers' families of origin, much of our creative programming and frantic organizing may be no more than rearranging deck chairs on the *Titanic*.[5]

The Helpless Parent

Even those Christian parents who start out intentionally nurturing the faith of their children often find that more "urgent" demands derail the priority of faith formation, as Merton and Irene Strommen's interview with this Christian couple indicates:

"Do we have family devotions?" Janet repeated the question after the interviewer. Then she looked over at her husband Bob and they exchanged a helpless laugh.

"I haven't heard that word for a long time," said the husband. "We had it when I was a kid."

"Don't you remember, Bob," said his wife, "we started out having something like that when the children were small?"

"Yeah, we were idealists, then, I guess."

"There are problems, aren't there?" The interviewer was tentative, waiting for a response.

"You bet there are," said Bob. "The last years I've traveled a lot in my business—days at a time, so Janet is alone with the kids."

Janet chimed in quickly. "I work part-time now, and when I get home, I'm a chauffeur. First I bring Betty to her cheerleader practice—it's every day after school, you know. John's in cub football now and then he'll have hockey. There's no time for *anything*, let alone something structured like family devotions. We scarcely eat together. I'm a short-order cook."

Bob was a bit meditative. "I can see where it would be a good thing. I hardly know what my kids are thinking anymore. But," and he gave that helpless little laugh again, "time is the problem. Time."[6]

Today's parents have become victims of their own schedules. They feel helpless—no longer in control of their own priorities. It is not surprising, then, that coordinators of Christian education programs across the country named the busy schedules of teenagers as only the second most common problem in Christian education. The most common problem was the busy schedules of adults.[7]

In our family of five, we have started the "regular" habit of family devotions more times than I can count. As the children get older and their schedules become increasingly complicated, the smallest diversion can throw our new habit off track. It is sometimes months down the road until we realign our priorities and start again.

This generation of parents seems to feel increasingly power-less over their children. Many parents have taken to heart the warnings of well-meaning friends, "You may enjoy your kids now, but just wait until they are teenagers!" The net result is that they are intimidated by the natural growth of their own children and paralyzed in setting priorities for them.

Like nervous drivers letting go of the wheel when something frightens them, many of these parents have "let go of the wheel" of giving guidance to their children. They simply close their eyes and hope they live through it. As Ben Patterson writes,

> Parents in the church today feel threatened and out of their depth when it comes to communicating the message of the Gospel to their children. They are not only insecure in their grasp of the Gospel, they are insecure in their grasp of their children. My congregation is filled with parents who would not dream of allowing their children to stay home from school because their children considered school boring. Yet they fold up when their kids tell them they think church is boring.[8]

Unfortunately, many parents have simply thrown up their hands in despair. These defeated parents may be among the 75 percent of letter writers who indicated to a newspaper columnist that if they could do it over again, they would not repeat the hassle of having a family.[9]

The Decline of the Family
The helpless parent syndrome is not caused primarily because of laziness on the part of the parents. These parents are products

of cultural forces that are just beginning to be acknowledged. Rutgers sociology professor David Popenoe has his finger on the pulse of the trends affecting the American family when he writes:

> During the past 25 years, family decline in the United States, as in other industrialized societies, has been both steeper and more alarming than during any other quarter century in our history. Although they may not use the term "decline," most family scholars now agree, with a growing tinge of pessimism, that the family during this period has undergone a social transformation. Some see "dramatic and unparalleled changes," while others call it "a veritable revolution."[10]

In an extensive collection of essays on the American family titled *Rebuilding the Nest,* editor David Blankenhorn discovered two noteworthy areas of general agreement among family scholars from a variety of different perspectives:

> 1. As a social institution, the family in America is increasingly less able to carry out its basic functions. The family, in short, is becoming weaker as an institution in our society.
>
> 2. The quality of life for America's children is declining. On this point, consensus really is the proper word. Scholarship tells us plainly that it is becoming harder each year to be a child in the United States. Surely, such an alarming fact should be widely known in our society. It is not.[11]

A youth worker can no longer say with integrity, "I was their age once." Certainly, we have been teenagers, but we have never had to face the kind of world that they face. Several summers ago, a Young Life camp offered a one-hour optional seminar entitled "Families in Crisis." Students were asked to come only if they were struggling with some difficult issue in their family and needed someone to talk to about it. The leaders had expected only a few teens to interrupt their free afternoon to come to the group. But for each of the four weeks of camp, the "Families in Crisis" seminar was packed out. Students told story after story of brokenness and crisis in their families. Hiding beneath the surface of these young people who looked like they had it all together was the incredible pain and fear that their families were falling apart.

The typical youth minister now works in a church where family values are embraced. But even in the most conservative churches, youth leaders deal with teens whose parents are openly having affairs, teens whose parents have committed suicide, teens whose parents are in prison, teens whose parents are alcoholics, sexaholics, workaholics and drug addicts. *Bankruptcy, embezzlement, court battles* and *custody dispute* are terms that are becoming more and more familiar to those called to Christian ministry with teenagers.

Newsweek's special issue *The 21st Century Family* suggested that between 1960 and 1986 the time a parent was able to spend with a child fell approximately ten to twelve hours per week.[12] The vacuum created by the frantic pace of the American family is filled by the electronic "value-neutral" nurture of television. As early as 1978 the *Saturday Review* cited the results of a two-year study in which a college researcher asked children ages four to six, "Which do you like better: TV or Daddy?" Forty-four percent preferred television![13]

A sign spotted in a toy shop window captures the attitude of hopeless confusion our culture has toward children and teenagers:

1920—spank them
1930—deprive them
1940—ignore them
1950—reason with them
1960—love them

1970—spank them lovingly

1980—to hell with them!

Although the jury is still out on what the nineties will bring, we can anticipate that the increasing speed of change will continue to place tremendous pressure on families.

The cumulative result of these changes has been that the tried-and-true formulas for parenting simply don't work any more. Kevin Huggins is right: "Any honest parent who is after more than outward appearances knows that formulas don't work. Detailed instructions are good for assembling toys; they're useless for raising kids."[14]

The Crisis as Opportunity

These cultural trends, though, do present churches with an unparalleled opportunity to impact entire families and thereby exponentially increase their ministry to teenagers. In my fifteen years of youth ministry, I have never seen parents more hungry for help than they are now. They want to spend more time with their children. They feel acutely the need to be better equipped as parents. As a result, the climate is ripe for parents to become increasingly involved in programs that can equip them in the spiritual formation of their children.

Why are these parents so desperate? They feel helpless, not only with their children but with their lives as a whole. For many parents, the years of parenting teenagers are by far the most stressful. As their children go through the developmental crisis of adolescence, many parents are experiencing an identity crisis of their own.

At its worst, this kind of parental desperation can be a nightmare for youth leaders. Parents who feel lost themselves and afraid of losing their children may blame the youth program for not doing enough.

But this desperation represents a teachable moment with parents that churches must not ignore. The popularization of the "dysfunctional family" phenomenon over the past decade has caused many adults to reconsider the mistakes and limitations of their own families of origin. Parents today, for the most part, are exceedingly interested in finding ways *not* to repeat the mistakes of their own parents. The vision of family-based youth ministry is to harness the incredible motivation of these parents and direct it toward solutions that can have lasting spiritual impact for their children.

In and of itself, the nuclear family is not enough, particularly in light of the tremendous pressures of our time. Every teenager needs an extended Christian family of significant adults. For the minority, that extended family will simply affirm the healthy Christian values they find at home. But for the majority, an extended Christian family is imperative to allow them to overcome the spiritual deficits of their family of origin. For many, the church may be the only Christian family they ever know.

Implications for Ministry

1. Nuclear families can play a significant role in the Christian nurture of teenagers in the church. But it is unrealistic to expect that all parents will be equipped and prepared, in and of themselves, to lead their children toward Christian maturity. Youth workers need to find ways to equip parents without basing the success or failure of the youth ministry on those parents' faithfulness.

2. During this season of tremendous motivation for parents to learn how to be more effective fathers and mothers, churches can seize the opportunity to help parents develop a Christian framework for their families and for their own lives.

3. Seminars on divorce recovery, preparing for parenting an

adolescent, marriage enrichment, teaching your children Christian values and understanding your teenager can all serve as windows to building faith maturity in the parents of teenagers.

Wild Hair—Create an "Introduction to Christian Parenting" class for all parents of sixth-graders to take just before their children become a part of the youth group.

Happy families are all alike; every unhappy family is unhappy in its own particular way.

LEO TOLSTOY, *Anna Karenina*

For young people, the home still ought to be the cradle of values, but unfortunately a staggering proportion of them do not live in stable homes. It is thoughtless beyond imagination for older people to say rigidly, "The child must learn his or her values at home," when there is no home. Some substitute must be found.

Religious training? It would be wonderful if every child had the warm, comforting experience I had in my Sunday School with its songs, its stories, its bags of candy at the holiday, but many are denied that. And while religion is an admirable teacher for those connected to it, it is a silent voice for those who are not.

JAMES MICHENER, *Life Magazine*

We don't really have a family. We just have four people who are making sure we all survive.

FIFTEEN-YEAR-OLD suburban church member

Today, for example, nearly one child in four in the United States is born outside of marriage, and the divorce rate in the United States is perhaps the highest in the world. Although the impact of this trend on adult happiness may be debatable, its impact on children's well-being is alarmingly clear—the mounting evidence of the harm done to children by divorce and unwed parenthood in our society has now become virtually unchallengeable.

DAVID BLANKENHORN, *Rebuilding the Nest*

If I grow up, I'd like to be a bus driver.

FIFTEEN-YEAR-OLD in a Chicago housing project

7
Beyond the Cleavers
The Challenge and Opportunity of Ministry to Nontraditional Families

One of the biggest occupational hazards for me in youth ministry is the telephone. Since the advent of the "Do Not Disturb" button on our church's phone system, I am longer a victim of calls that catch me at just the wrong time. But more recently, my trouble with the telephone has not been the calls that come to me but the calls that I make.

I know better. I tell myself over and over again that I know better. But on a fairly consistent basis, I find myself with a phone to my ear and a foot in my mouth. I dial the right number and ask for the wrong people—like when I call a twelve-year-old boy in the family by his sister's name.

But over the past ten years, my most classic phone faux pas (would that be "fauxn pas?") has gone something like this: My first call is to Colyer Anderson. As I expect, Colyer is not home, but I do get her mother on the phone. I am ready to seize the opportunity to build a little rapport with Colyer's mom. I look down on the list of parents' names in front of me to get her first name, and I respond pleasantly, professionally, "This is Mark DeVries at First Presbyterian Church. Is this Mary?" There is a long pause. There is an icy edge to her voice as she answers, "This is *not* Mary. Mary is Colyer's father's new wife. I am Betty Young, and how can I help you?" Talking around the size 10 shoe in my mouth, I leave my message as I fumble my way off the phone.

Besides giving me a crash course in phone etiquette for the nineties, these kinds of conversations serve as stark reminders of the increasingly complex home environments many of our teenagers grow up in. My first reaction to the growing number of young people in our church from nontraditional families was to create "niche" programs to reach each of the different kinds. It all started with a six-week divorce recovery course that went quite well. I began to think of all the possibilities: blended family support groups, chemical dependency groups or Twelve-Step groups of every possible variety. I even started a group just for teens who had been kicked out of school.

But after a year and a half of this diversified "niche" programming, I realized that this kind of strategy is simply unworkable over the long haul. First, this sort of "something-specific-for-everyone" style of programming requires a hefty budget and extensive manpower to maintain, even if the number of teens participating in each group is limited. This single factor keeps most churches from seriously considering this approach to reaching young people from "nontraditional" families. Second, those churches that take this route will quickly discover that teens from similar nontraditional situations do not fit neatly into groupings that can be sustained. Third, many young people from nontraditional families already feel sensitive about being "different." Emphasizing the different family "problems" may keep as many away as it attracts. And finally, it is next to impossible to design a program with enough "niches" for everyone in the group. Many young people will, by default, fall through the cracks.

Family-based youth ministry, therefore, is not about creating special programming for young people from each different kind of family. What every teenager needs in order to grow in Christ (that is, a faith-nurturing family and/or a faith-nurturing extended family) is true *especially* for those from nontraditional families. Need-centered programming may attract them to the youth program, but it will usually not provide them with the kind of foundational relationships with Christian adults that will lead to spiritual maturity.

Not All Bad News
Without a doubt, families today are far different from what they were a generation ago. But the changes in the North American family are not completely negative. Clearly, families in our time face increasing threats to their survival, but these threats may, in fact, strengthen some families as significantly as they destroy others.

In a recent "Preparing for Adolescence" class for parents of preteens, I began by asking the group, "Is it harder or easier being a parent now than it was for your parents?" Initially, the response was a unanimous, "Harder!" Then one reflective father said, "But my parents never had classes like these—and they needed them! It's harder for us, yes, but we've also got more opportunities to be trained, and we seem to be much more motivated to learn what to do differently."

There is a renewal of interest in learning parenting skills. And most parents have a healthy awareness of how little they really do know. The myriad of parenting materials available today only hints at the increasing desire that parents in the United States have to do their job well.

Here's some of the good news: The 1989 Mass Mutual American Family Values Study indicated that 81 percent of Americans view their family as a primary source of pleasure in their life.[1] And, in another study, 84 percent of men named "family" as the most important facet of their lives.[2] A recent *Time/Life* survey documented that today's fathers are investing *four to five times* the amount of time educating two children as their fathers spent raising five children.[3]

Not only are parents more interested in the family, teenagers seem to be as well. One survey asked young people aged thirteen to fifteen what they really wanted in life. Their number one desire was for a happy home life, and teenage boys indicated they wanted this even more than teenage girls.[4]

Five thousand high-school students were surveyed by the 1991 *World Almanac.* The students were asked "Who is your greatest hero?" Without even being included in the list of choices, "Mom" came in second, and "Dad" came in fourth![5]

In many ways, the more difficult and complex family life becomes, the more it seems to be valued by parents and children alike. I consider working with families at this time in our history to be an unparalleled opportunity for ministry. Parents and their children are increasingly interested in finding ways to connect with each other. And these connections can be the most crucial ingredients in the building of faith maturity in young people.

On the Other Hand . . .

Developing a ministry to teenagers from nontraditional families can be exceedingly difficult. Several years after I arrived in Nashville, I decided to "clean up" our rolls to find out the identity of the crowd I had never met. I found that the majority of the fifty young people who had been completely inactive came from families that had recently experienced some kind of major change like divorce, death or remarriage.

Recently I have analyzed the relationship between a young person's family situation and the likelihood of his or her involvement in our program. I discovered that teens who are living with both of their original parents are *two to six times* more likely to be involved in our church than young people who live with single parents or a stepparent.

When a teenager's family is in chaos, our creative newsletters and stimulating programs will not be enough. In this chapter, I want to identify the particular challenges that teenagers from various types of nontraditional families present to a youth ministry. The fact that I do not advocate special, diversified programming to reach these young people does not mean that we can ignore the unique demands of each teenager's home situation. Nontraditional families present a challenge to every church. And in general, young people from these families will require more support and attention (perhaps two to six times more) than young people from traditional two-parent families.

Types of Nontraditional Families

Divorce. When my parents divorced, I was just beginning junior high. At that time, it was still odd to be one of the few students who did not live with both parents. I can remember being embarrassed even to speak about it. Today, teens from divorced families may have lots of company, but they can still feel tremendously alone.

The divorce rate has begun to level out, but it has done so at an alarmingly high plateau: approximately 50 percent of marriages that begin this year will end in divorce.[6] Of the couples who divorce, approximately 70 percent have children under eighteen.[7]

Practically all recent studies of the effects of divorce on children indicate that there is, in the words of Andree Brooks, "frequently a substantial period of emotional and practical child neglect following parental separation."[8] The reasons are obvious.

First, the parents are preoccupied with their own issues of grief and anger and have less energy to attend to the needs of their children. Second, the economic adjustments that divorce almost always requires can often sap whatever nurture-giving energy a parent has left (the income for single parents drops an average of 37 percent within the first four months of the divorce).[9] Add to these reasons the chaos of a new routine of being transported from one "home" to another, and it becomes clear that children are often the biggest victims of divorce. The argument that divorce creates few problems for a child's long-term development is simply not consistent with the research in the field.[10]

Teenagers from divorced families often have extra demands placed on their time because of the multiple relationships that must now be maintained and because of adultlike responsibilities that must now be assumed. Because this time often competes with "church time," it is important that our youth ministries not abandon the young people who may need us most simply because they are unable to participate regularly in our programs.

In a recent extensive study of the effects of divorce on children, one fact stands out as a stark indictment to churches. *Under 10 percent* of those children of divorce who were interviewed "had any adult speak to them sympathetically as the divorce unfolded."[11]

Single-Parent Families. Approximately one out of every ten households is headed by a single parent.[12] Research also indicates that as many as 60 percent of children will spend at least some part of their childhood in a single-parent family.[13]

Often the more "family-centered" a church is, the more difficult it is for a single parent to find his or her place. When the majority of a church's groups and classes are designed for couples, it is easy to understand why so many single parents simply drop out altogether. When these single parents drop out of the church, their children almost always stay at home with them.

Although some single parents become incredibly intentional about bringing their children to church, many become sporadic in their own involvement, switching from one church to another many times in the span of a few years. This sort of inconsistency is particularly confusing for their children, who often choose to stay away from church rather than face the embarrassment of adjusting to a new group again.

Blended Families and Stepparents. When the two girls walked into the room together, they were noticeably tense. I greeted the girl I knew and asked her to introduce me to her friend. With an irritated sigh, she announced, "This is my dad's new wife's daughter" ("stepsister" was obviously too intimate).

Teenagers from blended families often carry around a subterranean tension that is seldom spoken and frequently left unresolved. Confusion and lack of clarity about parental roles often leave these young people with a feeling of being displaced in their own families.

The American Stepfamily Foundation reports that in 1990 one out of three children was living in a stepfamily.[14] These young people have an acute need for adult friends and the sort of identity that comes from being needed in the body of Christ.

Chemical Dependency. When a family member has a drug or alcohol problem, it affects all the other members of the family as well. Teenagers growing up in families with chemical problems almost always pick up some unhealthy relational patterns. The best hope for lasting change comes through sustained relationships with healthy adults who can help the young people see themselves and their family situation more clearly.

One way to help is offer quality "prevention" programming, but such programs, by and large, have a limited influence. These prevention courses can be greatly enhanced by involving the parents alongside their teenage children. Placing these programs in a parent-youth setting has three primary benefits:

1. Parents (even inactive parents) are concerned about these issues and are likely to attend and bring their children.

2. While the parents are focused on their children's high-risk behavior, they may be more open to changing their own inappropriate behavior.

3. While we talk about the issue, we involve parents and their children in community-building experiences that help to build an extended family for our teenagers.

Families Caring for Aging Grandparents. Many of the parents of our teenagers will be feeling the squeeze of working, raising children and caring for an aging parent at the same time.[15] Like most nontraditional family arrangements, having a grandparent in the home is a good news/bad news proposition. While the family benefits greatly from the grandparent's presence in the home, the parents, both of whom likely work full-time, find themselves increasingly exhausted with less energy to give to the intentional faith-nurturing of their children.

Kids in Poverty. Approximately 12 million children in the United States live in poverty, many of them in crime-ridden housing projects. Adult males are often conspicuously absent, and mothers, when they are not working, are frequently clinically depressed. More often than not the family structure has been destroyed, and children grow up with an inordinately high "accumulation of risk factors."[16]

Louis Sullivan's description of the kind of ministry that works with teenagers in urban areas sounds remarkably similar to the priorities of family-based youth ministry:

> It is time to remember what has worked throughout our history as African-Americans, a history of overcoming negative circumstances by the force of our character. And what worked was tight-knit families and strong neighborhoods supported by the community of faith.[17]

It is beyond the scope of this book and beyond the reach of my experience to speak in great detail about working with teenagers in poverty. But what I do know about working with children and teenagers in poor areas is that flash-in-the-pan youth programming has limited impact. The one determining factor for behavioral and academic success for young people from poor neighborhoods has been the level of stability of their families and extended families.

Both Parents Working and Busy Families. When both parents are working full-time outside the home, less energy and time are available for nurturing activities like talking, family meetings and eating together. In addition to parents working more hours away from their families, we have the increasingly hectic schedule of the children themselves to contend with.

It is easy for busy teenagers to relegate their faith to the category of just another "activity" or "program" to be added to their frantic lifestyle.[18]

Reaching Nontraditional Families

Families suffering financial reversals, families in which one member has a long-term terminal illness, families with foster children, families with a parent in prison, families with children with special needs and families with an emotionally absent parent will all pull teenagers away from traditional youth programming. Realistically, no one church can create a different educational program for each of the varying types of nontraditional families. What, then, can a church do?

Although the death of the traditional family has frequently been overstated (see appendix B), the fact still remains that approximately half the families in America can now be described as nontraditional.

There is the young person from the single-parent family who is uncomfortable around any group of peers. There is the boy from the Christian traditional family who has been arrested for stealing. There is the student whose parents are getting divorced who carries his Bible to school. And there is the girl from the missionary family who makes fun of anything remotely Christian. No neat and simple patterns.

The most effective strategy for reaching these young people is to provide a consistent personal ministry to each teenager who is a member of the church whether or not he or she ever attends. Admittedly, the building of this sort of personal mentoring program for each teenager requires a great deal of organization and follow-through, but probably no more time than most of us spend on our big programs like a youth week or the fall kickoff picnic.

The starting point of ministering to a generation of families that is "beyond the Cleavers" is recognizing that professional youth staff simply cannot do this work alone. There are too many families with complex needs. Each requires time that is above and beyond anything a single staff person or program can handle responsibly. As a general rule, programming will not be the key to reaching these youth. Relationships must be built in which their unique situation is understood and taken seriously.

The goal is to build extended families for our teenagers and their nuclear families so that the extended family, in turn, can provide the personal support necessary in each situation. More than anything else, what young people from nontraditional families need are roots into an extended Christian family that will "be there" for them, not simply a team of zany youth workers who provide short-term intimacy with little long-term support.

I am reminded of the company that went from making millions in profit one year to bankruptcy the next. The board of directors was puzzled, wondering, "We have done the exact same thing that put us at the top of our industry last year. What has happened this year?"

What "happened" was not caused by anything within the company. It had always run a great business making and selling bobby pins. But when the culture changed around them and hairstyles no longer required bobby pins, this company simply kept doing what it had always done. Because of a vision that was too small, this company folded.

As we approach the turn of the century, our world is undergoing enormous change. Families are changing. The teenagers we work with are becoming a new breed, different from any before them. Will our vision be large enough to meet these changes? Or will we wind up like the board of directors, scratching our heads, wondering why "doing it the way we've always done it" has left our ministries bankrupt?

Implications for Ministry

1. Because most young people from nontraditional families tend to "fall through the cracks" of a traditional youth program, ensuring that someone is available to administer the "trivial" task of keeping an accurate list of students' names, current addresses and phone numbers is absolutely essential.

2. Every young person needs contact from caring adults, but most teenagers from nontraditional families have an acute need for this kind of contact. The pastor or youth pastor can create a

system in which each young person is contacted at least once every six months simply to check in (the caller is sure to gain information about the family that would otherwise not be learned until the church's next stewardship drive!). If children from nontraditional families are two to six times more likely to stay uninvolved in our programs, perhaps God is calling us to give two to six times the amount of effort to reach them as we do to those who more naturally connect with the church.

3. It is crucial that young people from nontraditional families feel a part of the entire church and not simply a part of the youth program. Three ideas to build this kind of connection:

a. Youth leaders sit with students during worship on Sunday mornings in "big church."

b. Youth leaders or other adults in the church invite a teenager to all-church fellowship events (for example, Wednesday-night dinners).

c. Adults in the church invite teenagers to serve with them in local or out-of-town mission projects.

4. Design the publicity for programs in such a way that young people from nontraditional families get a personal invitation, a phone call or some extra reminder about the event.

Wild Hair—Cancel all youth activities (Sunday school, youth group, special events, Bible studies, retreats—everything) for one month to allow the youth leader to visit each young person.

• • • • • • • • • • • • • • • •

Somebody has to be crazy about the kid.

URIE BRONFENBRENNER, quoted in *Family Research Today*

Without a mentor, somebody who can kick around in a kid's head, talk to him about attitudes, about why he does what he does, about how important it is to meet other people halfway . . . a kid won't make it.

BRUCE RITTER, *Sometimes God Has a Kid's Face*

It takes the whole village to raise a child.

African proverb

It may well be that the sociological phenomenon that makes modern marriage [so] different . . . is . . . the attenuation of extended family connections. Even 2000 years ago the human institution of marriage would not have been able to carry the load of emotional satisfaction it is *expected* to bear today.

EDWIN FRIEDMAN, *Generation to Generation*

The youth ministries which will have the greatest impact in the coming revolution will be those which successfully recruit and equip lay people to bear the primary responsibility for reaching the current generation of junior and senior high school students.

MARK SENTER, *The Coming Revolution in Youth Ministry*

I still remember, as a junior high school student, refusing to go out with my friends on Friday nights because I would much rather stay home for my parents' neighborhood Bible study. I loved listening to them laugh and argue and study the Bible together. Surrounding your children with good people is one of the great gifts parents can give their children.

MIKE YACONELLI, *The Wittenburg Door*

8
Beyond the Teenage Family
The Power of the Extended Christian Family

L*ike most youth ministers, I get to attend more than my fair share* of high-school football games. Even though I have often been known to arrive at games shortly after half-time, when I climb into the stands it doesn't take long before I begin to cheer with the rest of the crowd. I get caught up in the spirit of the game, just as if I had been there from the opening kickoff.

I never made it far in my own football career. Twenty seconds of game time on the seventh- and eighth-grade teams was about the extent of my experience. By the time I got to high school, I had realized that football was no place for a 5'9", 110-pound class clown to shine; so I found my cheering crowd by being on stage. After hours of tedious rehearsals, I remember the energy of the opening night. The air became electric as the auditorium filled up. No dress rehearsal could compare to the thrill of the show with a real audience.

The author of the book of Hebrews understood the power of having an audience when he wrote, "Therefore, since we are surrounded by so great a cloud of witnesses, let us also lay aside every weight and the sin that clings so closely, and let us run with perseverance the race that is set before us" (Heb 12:1 NRSV).

Every Christian teenager needs an extended family of Christian adults—adults who can be a part of the "cloud of witnesses" that cheers him or her on. And the church should be the primary vehicle through which teenagers are exposed to the adults who make up their extended family in Christ.

What Is an Extended Christian Family?

An extended Christian family is a community of believers who affirm and encourage growth toward Christian maturity. Although having a set of peers who affirm one's Christian faith is important, teenagers particularly need adults who can help provide a consistent, lifelong structure of Christian maturity.

Apart from the family (and perhaps the television), the church may be the only lifelong nurturing structure left. Only the church and the family can provide Christian nurture from birth to old age and even death. All other communities (except, on very rare occasions, neighborhoods) are essentially orphaning structures (for example, parachurch groups, schools, scouts *and* youth groups).

Orphaning structures provide support and connection for people only so long as they fit into the age group of that particular organization. Many orphaning structures provide teenagers with a high degree of support and involvement. But, in the end, without the support of a lifelong nurturing structure, a young adult's life becomes fragmented and rootless.

Each time a person leaves an orphaning structures, he or she may feel confused and lost, looking for a new matrix for reality, a new place to belong. The rise in popularity of Twelve-Step groups reflects one way that disoriented people have been able to create for themselves lifetime support structures. Unfortunately, contemporary churches have been much more effective in providing young people with meaningful connections to the orphaning structure of the youth group than to the lifelong structure of the church. As Ben Patterson argues,

> It is a sad fact of life that often the stronger the youth program in the church, and the more deeply the young people of the church identify with it, the weaker the chances are that those same young people will remain in the church when they grow too old for the youth program. Why? Because the youth program has become a substitute for participation in the church. . . . When the kids outgrow the youth program, they also outgrow what they have known of the church.[1]

Wherever a mature Christian adult is found, chances are that a strong connection to an extended Christian family will be found as well. Sometimes even when the parents are antagonistic to the Christian faith, young Christians are able to continue to flourish in their faith. Almost always, this kind of growth happens not because of the charisma of a youth leader or the insight of a curriculum but because of a connection to an extended family that offers a different set of faith values.

My experience has been that a young person from a non-Christian home who makes a commitment to Christ through a traditional youth program winds up as one of three kinds of adults:

1. Many will simply reject their faith altogether as adults and follow the course of (non)faith set by their parents.

2. Others will make a connection to the adult extended Christian family of the church.

3. Interestingly enough, a sizable group will create their ex-

tended Christian family by becoming ministers themselves. For example, teenagers who come to know Christ through Young Life will often become Young Life leaders. New Christians who were nurtured in Campus Crusade will join Crusade staff. And the teenager who was nurtured in the youth group becomes a youth minister or marries one. Why? The primary Christian models for these young adults from non-Christian homes were Christian ministers.

The Extended Family's Impact Documented
There is considerable evidence to suggest that the kind of extended family that I have been speaking of has tremendous impact on the healthy development of a young person. Researchers at the University of California at San Francisco sought to determine why some young people are destroyed by the deficits of their home environment while others seem to thrive under the same set of circumstances. In reviewing these studies, Earl Palmer uncovered one constant factor among resilient teens:

> They all experienced the nonexploitive interest, care and support of at least one adult during their childhood years—a parent or grandparent, uncle or aunt, older brother or sister, coach or teacher, pastor or youth leader—an adult with no hidden agenda or exploitive design on the youngster.[2]

Several years ago, we began placing three or four adults in every Sunday-school class (usually with an average attendance of only ten students in each class). Many of the teachers and young people argued that it would be more efficient if we didn't have so many adults in the classes. But our goal is to expose young people not just to Christian teachings but also to real live adult Christians who call them by name and sit in the arena of faith to cheer them on. To provide our young people with an extended

Christian family gives our teens a resource pool of adults who can help them negotiate their own ideas and their own faith.

Benson discovered that "thrivers" have certain key assets that help them overcome adverse situations. And he heads his list of assets promoting resilience with "church or synagogue involvement."[3] Again, in *Children of Fast-Track Parents,* Brooks reports, "Studies of resiliency in children have shown time and again that the consistent emotional support of at least one loving adult can help [children] overcome all sorts of chaos and deprivation."[4]

Steven Bayme, director of Jewish Communal Affairs Department, documents the impact of the community of faith on the stability of Jewish families:

> More interestingly, among Jews affiliated with synagogal movements—Orthodoxy, Conservatism, and Reform—the chances of marriage ending in divorce are approximately one in eight. Among Jews unaffiliated with the Jewish community, the chances of divorce rise to one in three.[5]

Grandparents can also provide this kind of stabilizing influence for children. In his study of children of divorced parents, John Guidibaldi discovered that academic performance was significantly higher for young people whose grandparents lived close enough to be around to help out with household tasks. He found that the same positive academic results were typical of children who had regular contact with the relatives of their custodial parent.[6]

I remember Sunday lunches at my aunt's house with a table full of relatives, laughing and arguing around the table until it was time for supper. I remember a backpacking trip in Colorado with one high-school friend and four of our Young Life leaders. I can still recall the Sunday nights around the prayer altar at First United Methodist Church in Waco, Texas, with teenagers and little children and balding old men praying side by side.

Those experiences have filled my arena with a cloud of witnesses. In each of those settings, I was told in some way that my life mattered and that my faith was significant. Although I had a number of wonderful experiences with Christian friends who were my own age, none of them seem to have carried the long-term weight or given me the security that these connections with Christian adults did.

Of course it is only logical to believe that the best way to reach teenagers is creating a youth ministry. But in the long run, the teenagers in our churches will be impacted by significant experiences with adults much more than by the mountaintop youth group experiences that we spend so much energy creating.

The Shrinking Extended Family

Unfortunately, many of our young people run their race of faith in essentially empty arenas. Oh, there may be the fourth-grade Sunday-school teacher or the pastor from the town they used to live in, but for the most part, the stands are empty. In chapters two and three, I described the growing isolation of teenagers from the adult world. As teenagers are cut off from their extended families of support, they are abandoned to the much less healthy environment of peer dependence. It is no coincidence that the rise of the peer-centered youth culture has paralleled the shrinking of the extended family.

Glenn and Nelsen report, "In 1940, at least one grandparent was a full-time, active member of approximately 60 to 70 percent of all households. Today, fewer than 2 percent of our families have a grandparent available as a resource."[7] In addition, "the child culture [of a generation ago] consisted of interactions with siblings, cousins, friends, and classmates—children of all ages rather than age mates in a single peer group. In short, childhood in those days was an internship for life."[8]

But today, teenagers have less and less access to the natural extended family structures that lead to mature adulthood. They have such limited connection with adults that it has become a novelty for a teenager and an adult to have more than a passing conversation together.

Merton and Irene Strommen conducted a seminar for pastors on youth counseling a number of years ago. Part of the training involved the pastors' actively listening to a single teenager for forty-five minutes. The Strommens write,

> We were impressed by the fact that many friendships were formed between the pastors and youth, friendships that often continued through the years via letters. When several youths were queried about these friendships, one said, "You don't understand. Never before in my life have I had an adult listen to me for forty-five minutes. It's a good experience." We came to realize there are few times an adolescent is able to speak freely to an adult without being stopped short by a reprimand or correction.[9]

The Search Institute study indicated that under a third of the youth in mainline churches had felt the love and support of an adult in the church more than ten times over the past year.[10] What a tragedy that many of our young people have to pay an adult to listen to them!

A Great Idea!

The body of Christ is the extended family par excellence. From the birth of the church, Christians were called "brothers and sisters." Early believers understood that to be a Christian meant being involved in a new family. The extended Christian family (that is, the church) is not simply a safety net for those people who do not grow up in Christian homes. It is a new family which affirms and focuses our identity as believers. It is ludicrous to think that a person could be a Christian without being connected to Christ's body.

Marjorie Thompson's paradigm for faith nurture in the family firmly roots the Christian family in the larger context of the church when she says,

> It is inconceivable to treat the family as an insular unit, just as it is impossible to isolate an individual from the matrix of relationships shaping his or her individuality. The church is the context for our entire discussion of family spirituality. Without this context we will indeed reinforce the cultural idolatry of the nuclear family.[11]

Only in the church will young people move from the idealistic pseudo-faith of individualistic Christianity into the real world of following Christ alongside other imperfect people. I remember well how it felt coming home from my first Young Life camp as a teenager. How I wished the world could be like it was in Colorado—a world where everyone loved and listened to everyone else, a world where people didn't care what others looked like but loved them anyway, a world where everyone always got along. It took quite some time for me to realize that I would never find a church that was as wonderful as camp and that God was calling me to live through an often frustrating maze of relationships.

Mary Price Russell is a college student in North Carolina who grew up in our church in Nashville. When I first came here, she was the only active girl in a seventh-grade class of ten very active boys. Her parents have been intentional about nurturing their children's faith, making their home a place for gatherings of teenagers and adults alike. Mary Price is one of those young people who have grown to be "independent in Christ." She decided early on that she would not simply follow the faith of her parents, but would find her own way of knowing God. As a result, she frequently chose to attend another church, where she sang faithfully in the youth choir. She almost never came to our Sunday school and attended another youth group more than her own. On the surface, our ministry with Mary Price was a failure.

During her junior year in high school, she got into a typical, but explosive, argument with her parents. The argument was interrupted when she, in typical teenage style, grabbed the car keys and left. Of all the places she could have run, Mary Price chose to knock on the door of one of her old youth leaders from our church. Having someone who would listen to her and understand gave her the courage to return home. And because the youth leader was no stranger to the family, Mary Price invited him to return with her and help her say what she needed to say to her parents. Into the wee hours of the morning, the four of them talked and listened and cried their way to a renewed commitment to each other. Clearly, we had failed at getting Mary Price to come to our meetings, but we had succeeded in the more important task of surrounding her with significant relationships with mature Christian adults.

After high-school graduation, Mary Price joined a team from our church on a mission trip to Jamaica, where she experienced the body of Christ in even more vivid terms. On one day, she had stayed late with a few other teenagers to finish pouring concrete at the "infirmary" (which she described simply as "the place where people go to die"). As she waited for the bus, Mary Price talked with a old black man on crutches, who played song after song on the harmonica. As he finished playing "Amazing Grace," Mary Price and her new friend talked about their faith. Finally, she asked in her best Jamaican accent, "Bruce, Mon, you really do love the Big Guy, don't you?" As tears came to his eyes, he answered, "Price, Mom (Ma'am), today you are white and I am black. But someday," he pointed toward heaven, "someday, that will not matter, and we will be together."

Mary Price gained a priceless addition to her cloud of witnesses that day. She will never talk to this man again, but he has become a member of her extended Christian family. Her faith has been powerfully undergirded because of experiencing this adult from a very different world as a part of her extended family in Christ.

This past summer, Mary Price worked as a summer intern at our church. Coming full circle, she not only became part of the extended family for her students but also made it a priority to involve her class's parents as an extended family for her group. Her summer ended with an all-family picnic in her backyard with teens and parents laughing, eating and playing together. Mary Price understood how limited her impact would be unless she created a forum for the parents to be involved.

Stocking the Stands

Often the extended Christian family surprises our teenagers. They find, as Mary Price did, the serendipity of meeting some adult who validates their own faith experience. These experiences do not have to happen accidentally. We can actually create opportunities in which teenagers will be more likely to experience an extended family of mature Christian adults.

We have some friends whose six-year-old son recently made his own decision to follow Jesus. His parents asked him what adults he would like them to tell about his decision. He listed off the names of ten or twelve families, and now his parents have asked each of them to write him a letter (one letter a month) celebrating with him his decision to follow Christ. They want him to know that he now belongs to a much richer and larger Christian family.

In Peter L. Benson's recommendations from the recent

Search Institute study, he advocates that all youth-serving organizations find ways to "connect youth to adult mentors."[12] A number of Drug and Alcohol Abuse prevention organizations have designed a parental contract that creates a sort of extended family of support for positive values among teenagers. With very little effort, parents can be connected with other parents to affirm certain standards concerning curfew, drug and alcohol use, and serving drugs and alcohol in the home. With this sort of arrangement, teenagers are protected from their own ability to manipulate their parents with the "everybody else's parents are letting them do it" line.

Many churches have designed "Elder Friend" programs that match up young people being confirmed with one of the officers of the church. A friend of mine recently went through a very painful divorce. During the separation process, his teenage daughter ran away across the country to Colorado. When her father found out where she was, he realized that she was in the very town where the elder who had stood with the family at this child's baptism "happened" to live. Late one night, after receiving a phone call from his frightened daughter, my friend called across the country and said to this "elder friend," "Fifteen years ago, you stood with a little baby being baptized, and tonight she needs you."

This teenager had been involved in her church's youth program, but her experiences there pale in significance to the power of being connected to this mature Christian adult. This kind of connection gave her a lifelong nurturing structure, even when she had run away from her own Christian family.

If our youth ministries are going to have lasting impact, we must move away from our traditional model of placing highly programmed youth activities at the heart of our work. Instead, we must give a central place to the more significant ministry of connecting young people to their own "great cloud of witnesses."

Implications for Ministry

1. Establish a youth mentoring program that matches every one of the church's teenagers with an adult in the church.

2. Provide annual four-week courses for parents and teens together dealing with topics such as communication, decision-making, drugs and alcohol, sex, preparing for college, and so on. First Presbyterian Church in Nashville sponsors one of these courses for each class each year, allowing community to build over the years.

3. Strive to involve the parents of every young person in some volunteer capacity in the youth program during the year.

4. When teens take mission trips, commission them before the entire congregation as missionaries being sent out by the church.

Wild Hair—Have an Extended Family Scavenger Hunt or Road Rally during youth group one night. Each group would have a list of kinds of adults in the church to find (for example, an adult in the church whom you call by his or her first name, an adult in the church who knows the name of everyone in your family, an adult in the church whom you've never met but whose name you know). Teams load up in cars (driven by an adult, of course) to collect signatures from as many adults on the list as possible.

• • • • • • • • • • • • • • • • • •

Excuse me, if my parents like this shirt, can I return it?

TEENAGER, quoted in Kevin Leman, *Smart Kids, Stupid Choices*

Years of work with adolescents persuade me that they are the last ones in the world to want a freedom, a sense of privacy and autonomy that deprives them of the advice and counsel, the warm support and understanding of their parents, and, for that matter of others (teachers, doctors) who are older and might have a good deal to say about some of the difficulties that confront a person of 15, 16, or 17.

ROBERT COLES, *Sex and the American Teenager*

Interdependence is a higher value than independence.

STEPHEN COVEY, *Seven Habits of Highly Effective People*

The ancient Druids are said to have taken special interest in in-between things like mistletoe, which is neither quite a plant nor quite a tree, and mist, which is neither quite rain nor quite air. . . . They believed that in such things as those they were able to glimpse the mystery of two worlds at once.

Adolescents can have the same glimpse by looking in the full-length mirror on the back of the bathroom door.

FREDERICK BUECHNER, *Whistling in the Dark*

But you want so much to do something for yourself, by yourself, without your parents being involved, even if it's selling used cars. . . . A part of you wants to be totally different than your parents. But another part wants to be just like them.

TEENAGER, quoted in Andree Aelion Brooks, *Children of Fast-Track Parents*

Mere change is growth. Growth is the synthesis of change and continuity, and where there is not continuity there is no growth.

C. S. LEWIS, *Selected Literary Essays*

• • • • • • • • • • • • • • • •

9
Walking the Tightrope
Family-Based Youth Ministry and the Developmental Need for Independence

In my final year of seminary, I chose to focus my studies in the area of youth evangelism. Since there were no youth evangelism courses at my school, in many ways I had to start from scratch. I wound up writing to over a hundred professors, youth ministry organizations and denominational youth ministry offices looking for leads for information.

Responses varied widely. Organizations like Young Life and Youth for Christ were particularly helpful. They sent extensive materials used primarily in their staff training. Ironically, others wrote back simply to say that they didn't have time to respond to requests like mine (I did wonder where they found time to write me the note that told me they didn't have time to write me a note!).

But by far the most interesting response I received was from the director of the national youth ministry office of my own denomination. He wrote, "We are drawing the line and saying in areas such as evangelism it is high time that youth be significantly incorporated into the overall [adult] program and that there not be a special youth evangelism program."

Throughout this book, I have argued that youth do need to be incorporated into the total life of the church. I certainly have no problem with that perspective. What I do question is exactly *how* this "significant incorporation" will take place. The denominational executive's letter contains a noble sentiment—teenagers should be incorporated into the church beyond its youth ministry. But it doesn't take a rocket scientist to estimate how many teenagers actually *have been* "significantly incorporated" into their church's evangelism program through this kind of strategy. I would be so bold as to say that this kind of incorporation never happens unless adults intentionally plan for it. As Mark Senter's research highlights,

> A survey of the history of youth ministry shows that the evangelization of high school students, if left to peers, will never get done. Adults have consistently had to structure situations, train student evangelists, and hold the young people accountable to do the job.[1]

One church has designed its entire youth ministry around the no-intentional-plan philosophy. At this church, little or no money is budgeted for youth ministry (except, of course, to buy the denominational Sunday-school curriculum). The adults in the church throw up their hands when they talk about "kids these days" and are mystified to discover that so few of them show up for church. The minister and the church officers are particularly shocked and embarrassed to discover that their own children would rather go to Young Life than to the church.

What is this church doing right? Instead of isolating the youth into their own group, this church has expected young people to be incorporated into the total life of the church. But in their zeal for providing continuity and tradition for their teenagers, this church has neglected another equally important need—the adolescent need for individuation.

A second church's youth ministry is at the other end of the spectrum. This church has an active group of teenagers who are so distinct from the church that a casual observer would hardly recognize that they are from the same "family." The teenagers love being together, and they boast of significant numbers. Quite frankly, the church loves having so many visible teenagers; so when the youth break the rules on trips or at the church, the leadership has a habit of looking the other way. The classic response from the adults in the church is, "Let's not do anything that might make them leave!"

Wherever this group goes, their reputation follows them. They have done damage to hotels and retreat centers, performed dangerous "initiations" and learned to scoff at the rules other groups are expected to obey. This church has given its teenagers wonderful opportunities to "individuate" (separate from the tradition they have received), but they have been robbed of the continuity and accountability that comes from being connected to a community of faith.

What *Do* Teenagers Need?

One of the dads in our church hit the nail on the head when he described his fifteen-year-old son as "sometimes twenty and sometimes four." Teenagers frustrate us because they are caught somewhere in-between. And often they seem to be saying and showing that they need two very different things at the same time. They do.

If we design our ministries based exclusively on the expressed needs of our youth, we set ourselves up for frustration. Most (if not all) youth ministers have had the experience of asking a group of teenagers what they want to do, only to find (after hours of preparation) that the very ones who passionately pushed for the event decided not to come.

Rather than depending primarily on our teenagers' perceptions of what they want and need, it is our role as adults to know what their primary needs are and to create programs that will be responsive to those needs.

What, then, do teenagers need in order to grow toward mature Christian adulthood? Teenagers have a paradoxical task in faith development. On the one hand, they need continuity with tradition, a faith community to be nurtured in. But on the other hand, they need to step away from their inherited tradition and develop a faith of their own—not their mother's faith, the pastor's faith or their best friend's faith. These two tasks often seem to work against each other. But unless we address *both* of these needs, our youth ministries will be limited in their long-term effectiveness.

The Need for Continuity

Quite honestly, most "successful" youth ministries do a much better job addressing the need for individuation than responding to the need for continuity. Many youth workers revel in the fact that they are always in trouble for something, always questioning the status quo (although, in most places, teenagers do not need much help in rejecting the status quo!).

Johnny grew up in a youth group that was lacking in continuity. He hit our youth group running when he was in the seventh grade. *Intense* was the word we often used for him. Wherever our youth group was, Johnny was usually in the middle of it. He was a working machine on mission trips; he prayed with a passion; he sang worship songs with a serious spiritual intensity that I was thrilled to have in our group. I can still picture him in the back of the room at one of our "afterglow" gatherings after Sunday-night church, with his eyes closed tightly in worship.

Johnny was a model of following Christ for the others in the youth group. But as the years passed, and he graduated from high school and college, he began to understand his earlier intense spiritual experiences as something he did "when he was young." Although he still attends the same church sporadically today (as Johnny's parents did when he was growing up), he has lost the spiritual vibrancy that was so contagious when he was a teenager.

We were so busy keeping our youth ministry together that we failed to connect Johnny with normal Christian adults (youth leaders are typically not normal adults!) who followed God with a passion. I am not suggesting that the style of our youth ministry is the single most significant cause of Johnny's spiritual condition today. But I do know that, although we provided for many of his felt needs, we failed to address his need for continuity.

Recent studies are suggesting that teenagers may be much more open to experiences with their parents (and, by association, with other adults) than has commonly been believed. As a matter of fact, the first issue of the *Journal of Research on Adolescence* dispelled the myth that healthy adolescence requires a strong break with parents. Here are some of the conclusions:

1. Equating the youth years with inevitable storminess is inaccurate.

2. The predictable disintegration of parent-teen relationships (through conflicts) is also false.

3. Teenagers are more likely to support parental values than to be in conflict with them.[2]

Because the current of traditional youth ministry has been so heavily weighted on the individuation side of the balancing act, the majority of this book has emphasized the need for continuity. But on the other side of the tightrope is the teenagers' need for owning their own faith, for separating from and pushing against the tradition that has been given them. The remainder of this chapter will address that need.

Without this balance, a myopic emphasis on one need or the other can actually create rather than solve youth ministry problems. A new program overemphasizing continuity will be no more effective than the old one overemphasizing individuation. The "fall" is simply on the other side.

The Need for Individuation

Several years ago, I took a group of teenagers to Frontier Ranch, a Young Life property in Colorado. On the third day, right after breakfast, we were assigned to the ropes course, complete with zip line and high wire.

By the time I made it to the end of the course, I knew had a problem. I was still twenty-five feet in the air, and there was no logical way down. I couldn't go back. The two rugged freshman girls behind me would have laughed.

And then I saw it. Dangling in front of me, just out of reach, was a trapeze. Now I had read enough of those how-to-build-community-by-scaring-the-wits-out-of-kids books to know what was coming next. I was supposed to jump to the trapeze and trust that the sophomore boy holding the rope would not try to seek revenge for the wet willie I had given him that morning. (If you aren't familiar with the term *wet willie,* ask one of the youth in your church to demonstrate it for you!)

The instructor shouted up the simple directions, "Jump to the bar! It's the only way down!" As a Christian, I decided it was my duty to let the girls behind me go first. One at a time, they went. The girls leaped with no apparent concern for their bodies. I was less than eager to let go of my solid footing. There was no way to reach the trapeze and stand securely at the same time. Eventually, I did jump, caught the bar and was lowered to the ground without incident.

What a marvelous picture of adolescence! These are the "jumping-off" years. Some make the jump out of the security of childhood with relative ease. For others, it is a terrifying step. Safety harnesses (that is, parents and the extended family of the church) should be required equipment for everyone.

The Creator of the developmental process intentionally designed adolescents so that they would not be satisfied simply living as appendages of their parents. The story of Edsel Ford, the son of Henry Ford, is a classic example of the innate need children have to separate from their parents:

> The story of the life of Edsel Ford . . . is replete with examples of how Edsel was thwarted in this attempt [to individuate], turning finally to the world of modern art (something his father knew little about) as a way of distinguishing his life from that of his famous father. The need was so strong that Edsel continued to spend a great deal of his energies fostering modern artists even though the elder Ford scoffed at his endeavors, maintaining that Edsel needed nothing more than the chance to follow in his father's automaking footsteps.[3]

As Erik Erikson, David Elkind and others have argued, the primary developmental task of adolescence is the formulation of a personal identity. These "wet cement" years give us the most teachable moments for helping young people establish their own faith identities. These are the passionate years when teenagers "try on" different beliefs, like they might try on clothes at a department store. There is nothing healthy about teaching our teenagers simply to parrot back to us what *we* believe. If they are going to honestly embrace the Christian faith, they need to make intentional decisions about what *they* believe.

I am particularly grateful for "parachurch" groups like Young Life, Campus Life and the Fellowship of Christian Athletes, because they have consistently provided outlets for teenagers to express their own faith apart from the faith of their parents. Because these groups are seldom linked to a specific church and very few parents *force* their children to go to these groups, by attending, young people are often saying, "This is what *I* believe."

As a high-schooler, I was enthusiastically involved in a marvelous Young Life club. In my idealism, I expressed great frustration over the "deadness" of my own church (compared to the excitement of a Young Life meeting). There was even a time when I talked with my Young Life leader about starting our own church, because there were "no churches in town" that really seemed to understand what it meant to be a Christian. (Our wise leader, who was himself active in a local church, advised against it.)

At least part of my frustration with my church grew out of the passion of my growing relationship with Christ. Wisely, my "dead church" minister affirmed my growth and involvement in Young Life. His lack of defensiveness allowed me both to individuate and to maintain the necessary continuity with an extended Christian family in the church. Eugene Peterson's explanation matches my own experience: "Resistance to the church isn't the first step to atheism. It is more likely to be a natural development in discipleship."[4]

The fact that some teenagers seem to go along with everything their parents or youth leaders believe may be less a sign of maturity and more a sign of avoiding the challenges of growing up. Huggins points us beyond the pseudo-maturity of many young people when he explains,

> Too often the teens who find church attractive are the compliant/compulsive kids who possess the iron will to keep all

the rules that are given to them in the name of God. This is a tragic irony since the very thing that is supposed to be generating sole dependence on Christ is really strengthening a kid's dependence on himself.[5]

The Hazards of Individuation

Often the process of individuation is very uncomfortable for the keepers of the faith (parents and churches). Some teenagers arrive at their convictions only through a process of rejecting what they have been taught. Admittedly, much of this adolescent criticism and anger is immature, but for some it is a necessary step. If teenagers do not care enough about their faith to question their parents' or their church's beliefs, their faith will remain underdeveloped.

C. S. Lewis makes this same argument in *Miracles:*

Many a man, brought up in the glib profession of some shallow form of Christianity, who comes through reading Astronomy to realize for the first time how majestically indifferent most reality is to man, and who perhaps abandons his religion on that account, may at that moment be having his first genuinely Christian experience.[6]

And again, in *Mere Christianity,* he argues,

When a young man who has been going to church in a routine way honestly realizes that he does not believe in Christianity and stops going—provided he does it for honesty's sake and not just to annoy his parents—the spirit of Christ is probably nearer to him then than it ever was before.[7]

This dynamic poses a special predicament for the youth worker. It is possible that as we are successful in our work of moving youth toward mature Christian adulthood, we may very well find our youth become *more* critical of the church than before, because they care more. The process can be unnerving!

When I was a student at Baylor University (where I am told there are more Southern Baptists than there are people), I was at the height of my own spiritual individuation process. Everything was an issue worth arguing about. As I look back, I am amazed at how easily I could determine who was and who was not a Christian on campus (I had trouble finding even one Christian teacher!). As an older adolescent, I was able to know and affirm what I believed partly by clarifying who did and who did not believe like I did.

At its worst, this move toward individuation can become a judgmental "us versus them" battleground in which every issue is a witch-hunt worth burning someone for. But at its best, this experience can be a healthy part of establishing one's own faith. This process is *not* mature Christian adulthood, but it is often a necessary step along the way.

Jesus' methods for teaching his disciples addressed both their need for continuity and their need for individuation. Jesus did much of his teaching in the context of the religious establishment and quoted often from the Scriptures of the Hebrew tradition. But Jesus didn't teach his disciples by giving them answers that they could memorize but by raising questions that would engage them more deeply in the pursuit of God.

If we hope for our teenagers to grow toward mature Christian adulthood, we must stop programming in such a way that we exclude our best students—those who stay away from church because they care about their faith experience enough to question what they have been told. What is needed is a ministry that touches every teenager we are responsible for, whether or not they ever darken the doorway of our church. This kind of ministry will focus less on programming and more on intentionally helping young people build connections with mature Christian adults in the church.

Creating Opportunities for Individuation

Our youth ministries can encourage and support the process of individuation in several ways. To begin with, more of our programs can be designed for the youth themselves to serve and lead.

Giving real responsibility is the doorway into the world of adulthood. Research consistently indicates that when older youth tutor younger people, the tutors gain more from the experience than they give. The same is true in peer counseling programs. It is evident that when young people feel significant and needed, they tend to drop their delinquent behavior.[8]

Recently I had a mother explain to me that her son was unhappy because he was "not learning anything in Sunday school." When students and parents have complained about Sunday school in the past, my typical response has been to react by attempting to "fix" the class with some programmatic adjustment. Sometimes I would change teachers; other times, I would actually come and teach the class myself. But all my Sunday-school repair solutions met with limited success. By taking entire responsibility for the solution, I was part of the problem. I had failed to realize that my overfunctioning solutions created the dissatisfaction in the first place! So instead of trying to reinvent the Sunday-school program to keep this boy happy, I decided to offer him a position teaching alongside adults in a children's class.

Most churches have experienced the mass exodus of eleventh- and twelfth-graders from their youth groups. By the time teenagers are sixteen or seventeen, they will make one of two choices regarding the church: either they will become increasingly invested or they will drop out. Older youth in general will not continue being involved as spectators, regardless of how exciting the programs may be. In an age when teenagers are virtually unnecessary for the efficient functioning of society (and the church), we can intentionally create opportunities for our older teenagers to be needed.

A second way we can encourage our teenagers' process of individuation is to support their expressions of "moving away." The parents I respect most have made their children's church attendance a nonnegotiable but given their children the choice of what church they would like to attend. I have often said that some of the most mature teenagers from our church now go to other churches. I have to swallow my pride and give up my expectation that our program should be able to meet every young person's need. But, as startling as it sounds, without exception, I would have to say that our teenagers who have been active in other churches have gained more than they have missed and have grown in their faith. I take the same attitude toward our teenagers' involvement in Bible studies at school or Christian summer camps. Though their involvement in these groups may limit the amount of time they have for *our* youth group, this broader experience meets a specific need for our teenagers that exclusive involvement in our church youth group cannot meet.

My pastor in high school understood my need to participate in a variety of groups. He affirmed my involvement with a group of Young Life leaders who were much more conservative than he was. He asked questions and wanted to hear about my experiences, even if he couldn't agree with all the theological conclusions I was making.

A third way we can support this process is by creating multiple mentoring opportunities for all the teenagers in our church. Peter Benson's first recommendation to schools is easily transferable to the church setting. He advocates that schools become more "personaliz[ed] . . . so that each and every child feels cared for, supported and important."[9]

There are many young people in my church who have made the choice not to participate in our programs. But there are very few who would refuse an invitation to have lunch with me or with one of their leaders. By providing mentors for our youth, we can provide an extended family for our teenagers, whether they ever attend a youth event or not.

One final way to provide opportunities for teenagers to individuate is to plan for significant peer experiences for teenagers within the church. Without the foundational connections to mature Christian adults, this sort of peer-centered ministry can be no more than a short-term, flash-in-the-pan experience with no lasting impact. But with the proper foundation, teenagers can help each other significantly on their journey toward independence.

Adolescence involves letting go of the security that comes with dependence on parents. But teenagers are not fully prepared to be independent either. They need a handrail, something to hold onto until they become truly independent. Because teenagers are looking for a new family to which to give their loyalty, peers become a temporary family of sorts and, *in the short term,* can exert even more influence on their values than their parents do.

There is nothing wrong with using this positive peer pressure as a doorway into the church's program. Family-based youth ministry is not about abandoning traditional forms of youth programming as much as it is about building the foundation of solid connections with mature Christian adults.

Implications for Ministry

1. We can expect that as young people grow toward Christian maturity, some of them may very well go through a time of rejecting at least parts of the faith of their families before they can embrace it for themselves. If the church is prepared for this

type of response, they can, in a nonanxious way, continue to love and celebrate God's work in the young people who find themselves moving away from the faith they have received.

2. The natural adolescent desire for separation from the world of adults is a healthy, natural process. What is not healthy or natural is the neglect of teenagers by adults. We must not use the God-ordained process of identity formation as an excuse for the wholesale abandonment of our responsibility for the ongoing nurture of the next generation.

3. Youth programs that emphasize student leadership without connecting those teenagers to an ongoing community of faith deprive the young people of the very relationships that can most effectively lead them to Christian maturity. But undergirded by Christian families and the extended family of the church, those same student leadership programs can greatly enhance a young person's growth in Christ.

4. Many churches can easily hire an active senior to work five hours a week as an "intern" for the youth program.

Wild Hair—Cancel all youth activities for a month and allow each teenager in the group to find a ministry where he or she can serve in the church during that month. Report back at the end of the month and share ministry experiences.

And all the time . . . we continue to clamor for those very qualities we are rendering impossible. . . . We make men without chests and expect of them virtue and enterprise. We laugh at honor and are shocked to find traitors in our midst. We castrate and bid the gelding be fruitful.

C. S. LEWIS, *The Abolition of Man*

Entertainment reaches out to us where we are, puts on its show and then leaves us essentially unchanged, if a bit poorer in time and money. It does not (and usually does not claim to) offer us any new perspective on our lives or on other matters in creation.

DON MYERS, *All God's Children and Blue Suede Shoes*

The Church disowned, the tower overthrown,
the bells upturned, what have we to do
But stand with empty hands and palms upturned
in an age which advances progressively backwards?

T. S. ELIOT

All is summed up in the prayer which a young female human is said to have uttered recently: "O god, make me a normal twentieth century girl!" Thanks to our labors, this will mean increasingly, "Make me a minx, a moron, and a parasite."

SCREWTAPE (the tempter) in C. S. Lewis, *The Screwtape Letters*

The Christian home is a mission base when we refuse to "shop" for churches after one church has bored or inconvenienced us. This tendency betrays the blatant consumerization of our faith. When a family struggles to stay with a church through bad times, it demonstrates another way of life than that so relentlessly promoted by the economic exchange model.

RODNEY CLAPP, *Families at the Crossroads*

10
A Different Gospel
Youth Culture
Comes
to Church

I was twelve when I first visited the ocean. We went to visit family in Galveston, Texas, and arrived just in time for a brief swim in the gulf before the sun went down. My mother warned me that the ocean had strong undercurrents; and, much to my disappointment, she stood with a watchful eye, ensuring that I would not venture out more than knee deep. I promised myself that if I ever got back to the beach without her, things would be different.

When I got into high school, my brave pastor took four carloads of us (our total youth group and then some) to camp on the beach for a weekend. Even commando mosquitos, clingy sand and 100-degree-plus Texas weather could not spoil this trip for us.

The first morning at the beach, we let the adults set up a place we could call home base, and we threw ourselves at the waves with a passion. For hours, we played tackle the kid with the ball, king of the raft, and body surfing. Finally our stomachs screamed loudly enough to send us out of the water in search of food. As we walked to the shore, our group was nowhere to be found. We saw no home base, no familiar cars, no slightly overweight, sunburned pastor in sunglasses and Hush Puppies.

It didn't take long for us to realize that, while we were concentrating on having a good time, the current had carried us hundred of yards down the coast without our even knowing it. And because we were being carried along by the current, we didn't notice its strength.

In much the same way, the teenagers in our churches are being carried along by the strong currents of our culture and yet cannot feel it. Unless our youth programs work intentionally to resist these currents, our efforts at discipling youth may, in fact, simply entrench them more deeply in the very values that are in strongest opposition to the Christian gospel.

In this chapter, I want to identify three dominant currents of our culture which are more than simply a neutral cultural backdrop against which children in our time grow up. These are currents that can, in fact, push our young people *away from* maturity in general and from Christian maturity in particular.

All by Myself: The Conformity of Individualism

Recently, I was at a restaurant that is frequented by students from a local high school known for encouraging "nonconformity." As the students walked in, it didn't take me long to recognize all the students from that school. How could I tell? Every one of these "nonconformists" was dressed *alike*. Particularly striking were three senior boys with carbon-copy haircuts. They sat at their table with identical posture, manners and vocabulary. These students who prided themselves on their individualism did not have the power to resist the conformity that individualism always demands.

Although the individualist may live with the delusion of fierce independence, he or she is the most likely candidate for "codependence" or in Scott Peck's words, a "passive dependent personality disorder." Why?

Individualists, by definition, have freed themselves from loyalties that might in some way tie them down. But liberation from all loyalties beyond self cuts a person off from roots that bring the stability and identity necessary to stand against the currents of our culture. The idea that deep within each one of us there is a "genuine" self completely separate from our roles and relationships is nonsense. If you take away my roles as husband and father and Christian and pastor and friend, there isn't any private self to discover! As Robert Bellah explains, "My 'self' is composed of my relationships and commitments, my 'roles,' if you will. That doesn't mean I lack autonomy. Indeed, only because of my relationships and commitments can I be autonomous at all. If I were isolated, I would be helpless."[1]

Some rejoice over the "return to traditional family values" in our culture. Realistically, this trend must be understood as one more phase in the evolving conformity of individualism. After all, family values are "in" these days. We would be unwise to get our hopes up. This too shall pass.

The persistent current of individualism has radically changed the character of the American family. Carl Schneider in the *Michigan Law Review* has observed that family members today tend to view themselves "as a collection of individuals united temporarily for their mutual convenience and armed with rights against each other."[2]

Individualistic Christians, carried along more by the culture than by the gospel, have come to define all their commitments in terms of *self*-realization: marriage is seen as personal development; work as personal advancement; and church as personal fulfillment.[3] When asked why they attend church, the individualist response is always, "Because I get something out of it." Christian individualists learn to approach God as a doting old grandfather, a "mush god," perhaps a cross between Big Bird and Mr. Rogers—the kind of friend who would never say no. It is this sort of understanding of God that led a college girl to argue vehemently, *"My* Jesus wouldn't think it was wrong for me to sleep with my boyfriend!" And it is this kind of understanding of God that leads musicians who use blatantly immoral lyrics to "thank God" when they receive a Grammy award. Christians carried along by the current of individualism cannot help but create God in their own image.

Several years ago, Vanderbilt beat the University of Tennessee in a barn-burning, buzzer-beater basketball game. One of our students from Vanderbilt made sure he called his father (a UT graduate) to gloat over the game. The father's only comeback was, "You have to admit that UT did have the strongest single player on the court." The son quickly responded, "Yeah, Dad, maybe that player needs to take up tennis. Basketball is a team sport!" Christian discipleship is a team sport. It always happens in the context of Christian community.

One of the goals for our youth ministry is that our teenagers will grow to become "independent in Christ," that they will be able to stand alone when their faith calls them to do so. But there is a clear distinction between healthy independence and the (unhealthy) cultural current of individualism.

An independent person has the power to "say no" because his or her identity is grounded in a heritage of secure relationships. The individualist can only do what he or she wants.

The independent person is secure enough to serve or give without being consumed in the process. Individualists (whose only identity is in themselves) will become consumed in validating their identity and proving their worth through serving, achievements, relationships and activity.

Todd is an independent college student who still calls his parents his "heroes." He was deeply involved in our youth ministry before going off to college and developed strong connections with a number of Christian adults. During high school, he attended a boys' school in which short hair, khakis and button-down oxford shirts were the accepted dress. But Todd chose to grow his hair long (quite a creative accomplishment at a school where the hair must be off the ears and off the collar!) and wear clothes quite different from those of his peers. Although he chose never to experiment with alcohol or drugs, many teenagers and their parents looked on him as an amoral "druggie." His poetry only hints at the courage he developed on his journey toward independence:

No one wants to hear
My inner song
"Smoke your dope, boy,
Your hair is long" . . .

Breaking stereotypes
Would use your mind
Are you afraid of character
You might find?

When the majority sins
Nobody cares
Just lynch the different
The ones who dare
For your bigotry

There is a season
Clean image complements
Your moral treason.

With feet firmly planted in his family and his extended family, Todd had the courage to stand against the crowd.

Churches that are carried along by the current of individualism can inadvertently train teenagers that being a Christian is primarily a personal and individual affair. The unspoken message to many teens involved in these churches is that their personal faith decisions are all that really matter. This belief is found most notably in the scores of young adults who argue, "I don't need to go to church to be a Christian."

I have often wondered what would happen if football coaches approached their work like most youth ministers are expected to. For example, I wonder what would happen if when a player was too busy to show up for practice, the understanding coach simply said, "We'll miss you. I hope you'll be able to make it next week sometime." Imagine the players leaving practice and hearing the smiling coach say, "Thanks for coming. I hope you'll come back tomorrow."

If a football team operated like a typical youth ministry, we might expect concerned parents to call the coach, saying, "Can you tell me what's been going on in practice? My son says it's boring, and he doesn't want to come anymore. I was wondering, could you make it a little more fun for them? And by the way, you might want to talk to the coach at the school across town. He seems to have the right idea." The coach might send out quarterly questionnaires about what the players would like to change about the team (I can just imagine the answers: "shorter practices," "more winning").

A coach, responding like a typical youth minister, might first feel guilty that the practices were not meeting the boy's needs, and he would try to adjust his program to suit this boy (and every other boy who complained). Between trying to keep everybody happy and giving every student a good experience, the coach would squeeze in a little football practice. And what kind of season would this coach have? It's a safe bet that the coach wouldn't be the only one who felt like a loser.

But this is the very way that most churches expect to run their youth ministries. To expect that youth be committed to the church at the same level of commitment that would be expected on an athletic team would draw the charge of legalism and insensitivity. Our culture has been so carried away by the current of religious individualism that the expectation of commitment to the church has become implausible to most Christian parents. Because the god of individualism pressures us to program to the lowest common denominator, we seldom raise the expectations high enough for teenagers to experience real community.

Real community means real responsibility for each other. It means a commitment to be there for each other even when the schedule is tight and when motivation is low. But the typical Christian adult in our culture knows little about commitment to community.

In our city, there are five prominent evangelical churches. Like good individualists, many of their members move among the churches as easily as they change their clothes. When they feel the need for a little more liturgy, they move to the charismatic Episcopal church. When they are looking for a little more freedom in worship, they move to the fast and loose Pentecostal church. In the mood for more substantive teaching? The conservative Presbyterian church will do the trick. For these enthusiastic Christians, loyalty to a specific community (which can often be quite bothersome) is rejected in favor of finding a place that "meets my needs."

Most youth ministers have their files jam-packed with lessons that promise to help build young people's self-esteem. But positive self-esteem is gained by repeated interactions with others who have gone before, by affirmation from and connection to a genuine community.

If we hope to move our young people toward mature Christian adulthood, the discipline of community needs to be a central focus of our program. Our teens' spiritual maturity will be limited if our teaching and programs center exclusively on personal, individual faith. If all they experience is this kind of teaching, chances are they will simply grow fat without growing strong.

Can We Change the Channel?

One of the favorite images of the late 1980s was the "couch potato," a person spending his or her life on the couch watching television, experiencing everything secondhand. Couch potatoes sit, wait and react. When they get bored, they simply change the channel to something more exciting.

Through consumer-oriented entertainment, our teens have been conditioned to seek pleasure (or the avoidance of pain) as a goal for life. From kids who lick slimy secretions from toads to get high[4] to others who wear the "party till you puke" philosophy plastered all over their lives, pleasure has become serious business.

A group of teenagers was asked recently, "What images come to mind for the word 'party' when you think of your peers?" The response: "Keg of beer, drugs, sex, loud music, getting destroyed, totaled, wasted, hammered, annihilated, decimated."[5] What caught my attention about this study was not the typical teenage responses but the way that teenagers describe their images of "partying" in *passive* terms. These descriptions indicate that teens perceive "fun" as something that happens *to* them.

Next to sleeping, the teenagers that we work with will spend more time watching television than pursuing any other activity. Is it any wonder that approximately three-fourths of the teenagers surveyed in the Search Institute study indicated that they thought church was boring?[6]

I don't know of any youth ministry that can, week in and week out, compete with a 92-million-dollar movie. Compared to most other options young people have for entertainment, we don't have a chance. If we train our youth to expect entertainment from church, we can be assured that when things get a little slow, they will be switching the channel to somebody else's show.

A 1989 Gallup poll discovered that 95 percent of teenagers believe in at least one supernatural phenomenon (for example, angels, astrology, Bigfoot, ESP, witchcraft, ghosts, clairvoyance or the Loch Ness Monster).[7] And why not? These beliefs require no investment or commitment. They can simply be held passively without any risk or involvement.

Entertainment-centered programs provide an artificial intimacy, like a crowd at a concert, without the joys or frustrations of real relationships. But when drawing teens through exciting programs becomes the goal of a youth ministry, we are in danger of teaching them that the Christian life will always be a party. Some Christian sociologists have called this generation of Christian youth "God's little brats." They are growing up with the expectation that they should never be bored, never be uncomfortable, never have to do without.

I have discovered an interesting phenomenon. Often the most spiritually responsible adults have come from miserable "youth programs" where there was no youth pastor to blame for the problems in the group. These young people and their parents had to take responsibility for their youth ministries. They have had to struggle with failed attempts to get a program off the ground. These young adults are often the best prepared to live a Christian life that doesn't get neatly fixed in thirty-minute blocks.

Youth ministries that are carried along by the current of entertainment will treat their youth as consumers, and the leadership will do everything it can to "keep the customer happy." This fact may explain why the majority of *churched* teenagers do not know why Christians celebrate Easter and cannot even name the four Gospels. Learning the basics of the Christian life takes work and discipline (the very demands that just might keep youth away!).

Most churched teenagers have just enough knowledge of the gospel to inoculate them against ever being transformed by the it. They know bits and pieces of the biblical story, but they know the Disney myths much better (every one of them could tell you what happened after the Handsome Prince kissed Sleeping Beauty, but few know what Abraham, Isaac and a knife were doing on the mountain together!).

Young people who develop a low tolerance for boredom will be unable to practice the disciplines necessary to grow in the Christian life. Prayer, Bible study, fellowship, witnessing, fasting and solitude are all disciplines that have at their very heart the facing of our own boredom and restlessness.

Looking Good: The Cultural Demand for Success

A 1991 report described the results of cross-cultural study designed to determine the prime causes for misbehavior in adolescents. Researchers identified two "universal factors associated with misconduct." Not surprisingly, the first was the level of parental monitoring (that is, limited parental participation was a likely indicator of misconduct). The second factor was more surprising.

The study showed that the more a teenager valued "outward success," the more likely it would be for that teenager to misbehave. Youth in each of the three countries studied (U.S.A., Australia and Hong Kong) all reported the same trend. Values like wealth, power, a comfortable life and social recognition were strong predictors of misconduct.[8]

In this culture where human value is often reduced to how much one produces, teenagers are often seduced into bowing down before the false god of success. But, as the research indicates, teaching our young people to place a high value on success does not always have positive consequences.

James Dobson, in his classic book *Preparing for Adolescence*, describes how teenagers are often victims of a cultural system that tells them they are valuable *if* they are physically attractive, *if* they are intelligent or *if* they have money.[9] As long as young people depend on these visible signs of success for their self-esteem, they remain dependent and immature.

Henri Nouwen was a highly respected professor at an Ivy League university. Having written a number of bestselling books on Christian theology, he was a sought-after lecturer, a man of no small stature in his field. His convictions about the nature of the Christian faith, though, led him to leave his prestigious position and join the staff of an institution that cared for adults with mental disabilities.

In his new position, no one recognized him as anyone "special" except in that he was a part of their community. Nouwen's move represented his refusal to allow his identity before God to be tied up in his ability to perform or produce or succeed. He explains,

> It seems easier to be God than to love God, easier to control people than to love people. . . . The leader of the future will

be the one who dares to claim his irrelevance in the contemporary world as a divine vocation that allows him or her to enter into a deep solidarity with the anguish underlying all the glitter and success and bring the light of Jesus there.[10]

For Christians, measurable success can never be our primary goal. Judas was looking for visible signs of Jesus' success. The Pharisees demanded signs to prove that Jesus was speaking the truth. But, according to the New Testament, Jesus never did anything to build a crowd. As a matter of fact, he often tried to do just the opposite. Visible signs of success were not high on his priority list.

If we place success over faithfulness, we will inevitably choose image over substance, in danger of becoming ecclesiastical public relations directors rather than ministers of the gospel.

One of the college students who works with our teenagers was asked by some parents, "What are you going to do when you graduate from Vanderbilt?" He explained that he was considering full-time ministry with teenagers. Later, I couldn't believe what I happened to overhear. One of the mothers in our church said, "How can he do that to his parents after all the money they put into his education?" Image over substance.

Youth ministries teach young people that success is the real priority when they only use good-looking adults for youth leaders. We train them to seek success first when we consistently recognize those who visibly accomplish the most. We demonstrate how highly we value success when the youth minister cannot "handle" having a program that fails. Our young people may learn more about discipleship by watching their leaders struggle than by following the seemingly magical gurus who find success second nature.

Young people do not need our help in learning how to handle success. They need training in living with failure. All the great success stories I know of have more failures in them than successes. Abraham Lincoln, Louis Pasteur and Martin Luther are known for their success but faced failure over and over again. And I'm told that every great songwriter in Nashville has a much larger trash pile than "hit" pile.

When our youth ministries tacitly teach the doctrine of success, first, we are in danger of raising a generation so afraid to fail that they are paralyzed to take the risks necessary to live the abundant Christian life. When the young people leave our meetings thinking, "Those guys are so good. How do they do it? I could never do anything like that!" we have taught them not to risk, because to do so could mean they wouldn't measure up.

Youth who graduate from a success-centered youth program learn to treat God as the most efficient means to their success in life. They learn to pray because "it works" or because "it makes me feel better." These young people grow up to be adults who are surprised by struggles and wonder how a loving God could ever let them suffer or fail.

A ministry that is leading teens to mature Christian adulthood will often find itself going against the stream of these values. I picture the forces of youth culture as in figure 3.

The diagram is most easily understood as a canal through which a child's faith "flows" toward maturity. The thesis of family-based youth ministry is that the family and the extended family of the church are the structures (or walls of the canal) that most naturally move a person toward faith maturity. As a teenager moves into adulthood, the extended family of the church will begin to have the most formative influence on a young person's faith. The primary task of a family-based youth ministry is to "pass the baton" of faith formation to the extended family of the church. Because traditional youth ministry takes place outside these structures, young people in those ministries are more susceptible to the juvenilizing forces of youth culture.

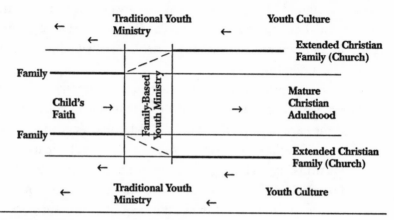

Figure 3. The Forces of Youth Culture

Implications for Ministry

1. The only way to combat the encumbering influences of modern youth culture is to connect teens to adults who are moving against the culture. These relationships can give young people courage as they go against the flow.

2. It is very appropriate for leaders to ask the young people in their groups to be as committed to the community of faith as they are to an athletic team (for example, showing up for practice even when they don't feel like it).

3. Churches can invite interested teens to participate in community spiritual disciplines that allow them to face their boredom and not run away from it (for example, fasting, concerts of prayer, days of silence).

Wild Hair—Have an Annual Boredom Fest—a night when everyone is together with nothing planned, no games planned, no materials (like pool tables or Ping-Pong tables). Or take a year to enjoy (as a youth group) another church's Sunday-night programs rather than taking time to plan something new each week.

• • • • • • • • • • • • • • • • • • • •

It is not within our power to place the divine teachings directly in someone else's heart. All that we can do is place them on the surface of the heart so that when the heart breaks they will drop in.

Hasidic Saying

Question: What is the chief end of man?
Answer: Man's chief end is to glorify God and enjoy him forever.

Westminster Catechism

Cursed is the one who trusts in man,
who depends on flesh for his strength
and whose heart turns away from the LORD.

Jeremiah 17:5

God may be one, but it takes two to find him.

MARTIN BUBER

God has so ordained things that we grow in faith only through the frail instrumentality of one another.

JOHN OF THE CROSS, 16th century

As long as ministry only means that we worry a lot about people and their problems; as long as it means an endless number of activities which we can hardly coordinate, we are still very much dependent on our own narrow and anxious heart. But when our worries are led to the heart of God and there become prayer, then ministry and prayer become two manifestations of the same all-embracing love of God.

HENRI NOUWEN, *The Way of the Heart*

The kingdom and the reality of church as first family deny the right of biological family to be the whole world for any of its members. For of course any family tht attempts to be the world for itself in fact creates a stunted, shrunken world. Paradoxically, a family is enriched when it is decentered, relativized, recognized as less than an absolute.

RODNEY CLAPP, *Families at the Crossroads*

11
God Calling
Thinking Theologically About Youth Ministry

We spent most of our lunch together talking about how to make our youth ministry work. After an hour and a half and five glasses of iced tea, we ended our conversation enthusiastically, both convinced that our new design was going to increase vastly the scope of our ministry. As a father of three teenagers himself, my lunch partner had been actively supportive of our work. He was a faithful giver to the church and a diligent student of the Bible. As we walked out the restaurant together, I was grateful to have someone like this man on our team.

But before we reached our cars, he stopped, suddenly very serious, looked me in the eye and said, "You realize that if this program is going to work, it is going to have to be *flawless.*"

I wasn't quite sure how to respond. At first, I generally agreed, mentioning something about how important it was for us to be faithful with our plans. But then my honesty slipped out: "I do need you to know up front that I am not particularly into perfection."

He looked at me like I had just flown in from Mars. "What do you mean?"

I explained, "I don't believe the level of our program's perfection is going to make or break our youth ministry." I read his blank stare as an invitation for me to continue. "As I see it, the Christian faith is not about our perfection but about God working through our imperfection and even our failure. That is the whole idea of grace."

His brows furrowed as he searched for a response. Finally, in frustration, he blurted out, "Look, don't bring God into this. We're talking about our youth program here!"

I understand that many Christians (ministers in particular) can be guilty of avoiding responsibility by theologizing from their ivory tower, and so I understand what my friend was getting at. But I'm afraid that much of our thinking and planning about youth ministry is done outside the context of our faith. And when dependence on God's grace is excluded from our thinking, we wind up trusting our human strategies (and our own ability to work those strategies) more than we trust God to work through us.

A Place to Begin

One of my foundational theological assumptions is that we never quite "get it right" when it comes to understanding God. All our language, all our descriptions, are provisional. No matter how well we understand God today, there is a fuller understanding still awaiting us. With this disclaimer as a context, I want to offer in this chapter a "first draft" of a brief theological foundation for family-based youth ministry.

As we think theologically about the process of helping teenagers move toward mature Christian adulthood, we must begin with God's central role. We begin with a confession that all of our methods, all of our programs, all of our systems are not enough to lead a young person to genuine repentance and faith.

Our goal is not simply to socialize young people into the faith, as if somehow, by finding the right production method, we could mass-produce mature Christians. We must not delude ourselves into thinking that we can "make" teenagers into anything, particularly mature Christians. What we can do is provide a context in which they can, to borrow Eugene Peterson's wonderful expression, "acquire a taste for grace."

We have no more power to make a young person grow faith than we have to make a bean sprout grow. All we can do is plant and water. We cannot get down inside the seed and pull out a plant. We can simply do the very small, but important, part of planting and nurturing the seed.

To use another image, a doctor can only bandage and set a broken bone. The physician cannot make the bones grow back together. All he or she can do is work with God's healing process. In other words, *we* will never be "successful" in making young people become mature Christian adults. But we can work with God's process to support them in the growth that only God can bring. In this sense we do not "take Christ to kids." But we do have the privilege of being included in God's revelation of himself to them.

Only when we understand that we, as well as the teenagers we seek to reach, are "under God's grace" will we ever be free from the driven hyperactivity that has become typical of so many youth ministries. God uses us most often *in spite of* our gifts, abilities and hard work, not because of them.

Perhaps this fact is the reason Jesus sent out his disciples empty-handed. He warned them, "I am sending you out like sheep among wolves" (Mt 10:16). Sheep are defenseless. No matter how many push-ups they do, no matter how much training they have, in a head-on battle with a wolf, a sheep will lose every time. As long as the sheep is depending on its own resources, it can never win.

Jesus introduces this "sheep among wolves" warning by reminding his disciples of the uselessness of any human strategy they might be tempted to depend on. First Jesus tells them, "Do not take along any gold or silver or copper in your belts." A sheep with a bigger budget is still powerless against wolves. We cannot buy victory in the battle to which we have been called. Next Jesus instructs his disciples not to take a bag or even a second coat or shoes. There is no bag of tricks big enough for a sheep's encounter with a wolf. In Christian ministry, there is no human resource sufficient for the task, no provision for what to do when what we have wears out.

Those things we would instinctively reach for to support ourselves (like perfection, hard work and the best human strategy) will not guarantee the effectiveness of our ministries. A generous youth ministry budget, all the right connections, even our bag of methodological and perfectionist tricks will not be enough to ensure our success. The Shepherd offers his sheep no provision other than himself.

Ministry by God's Design

Recognizing God's central role in our ministries (or better yet, our supporting role in God's ministry), the best we can do is to work *with* God's design for faith formation. God's first provision for faith-building is the family. The famous words of the Shema remind us of the primacy of family and extended family relationships in faith-shaping:

Hear, O Israel: The LORD our God, the LORD is one. Love the

LORD your God with all your heart and with all your soul and
with all your strength. These commandments that I give you
today are to be upon your hearts. Impress them on your
children. Talk about them when you sit at home and when you
walk along the road, when you lie down and when you get up.
. . . Write them on the doorframes of your houses and on your
gates. (Deut 6:4-9)

God's provision for the Christian nurture of children begins with
families. No mention is made in this text of the priests taking
responsibility! These early parents (and their Israelite kin) were
not told to get their children to meetings or to worship (that was
understood). They were commanded, instead, to talk about God
and his commands throughout their daily activities.

For most Christian teenagers, Sunday school and youth group
have become a substitute for religious training in the home.
Interestingly enough, the Sunday-school movement itself began
as an outreach to *unchurched* poor children. Its founders never
intended for it to take over the role of Christian parents.

In many ways, family-based youth ministry is not a "new"
model as much as a return to God's original design. Christian
educator John Westerhoff affirms, "No matter where you look in
our Judeo-Christian heritage it is the parents who have the prime
responsibility to bring up their children in the faith."[1]

There is a "table spirituality" that is central to the Christian
faith. From the Jewish family rituals of the Passover and the
sabbath to the Lord's Supper and even to the "banqueting table"
of our Lord in heaven, the undercurrent of a family meal is
consistent. When women came to Jesus asking him to bless their
children, Jesus could have sent Judas off to start a "Kids' Klub"
program for them. Instead Jesus held them in his arms and
blessed them.

It is startling to realize the lack of programmatic focus in Jesus' ministry. He had no organizational chart, no planning team, no curriculum, no ten-year long-range mission statement. Jesus' first priority in calling his disciples was "that they might be with him" (Mk 3:14). Jesus' ministry was relational rather than programmatic, more like a father's plans for his children than a CEO's designs for his or her company.

The Disciplines of Community

As I suggested in the last chapter, much of popular religion in our country today has taken on an individualistic emphasis. Scott Peck in *The Road Less Traveled* argues, "The ultimate goal of life remains the spiritual growth of the individual, the solitary peaks that can only be climbed alone."[2] Certainly, the spiritual growth of the individual is an important *part* of the Christian vocation, and often God does call us to stand alone. But the personal growth of the individual Christian cannot be our ultimate goal. This is the very issue that the Westminster Catechism speaks to in its first question.

Question: What is the chief end of man?

Answer: Man's chief end is to glorify God and enjoy him forever.

As disciples of Christ, our ultimate goal ("chief end") is not limited to our own personal growth. That goal is much too small. The glory of God comes first for the Christian. Our enjoyment of God and our own spiritual growth are a natural outgrowth of learning to give God the glory that he deserves.

In the New Testament I find no recorded incidents of God dealing with his people in isolation, simply as individuals. Even Jesus surrounded himself with twelve stiff-necked men. After Saul received the revelation from Jesus on the road to Damascus, Jesus directed him to another person, Ananias, to complete the transaction. Of course, Jesus could have simply given Paul instructions for his future ministry and sent him on his way. But instead, God's design was to connect Paul to the community of faith.

From the very beginning of his ministry, Paul was involved with other Christians. When he started churches, he assumed that all believers would be committed to the body of believers in that community. There was no hint of salvation without a link to a specific community of faith. When Paul went to make disciples, he could have held evangelistic crusades, inviting people to "get right with God." But instead, he planted churches. Apparently, he understood that the nature of the life of discipleship involves a practical commitment to a specific community of faith.

Whether churches practice infant baptism or infant dedication, almost always two groups of people in the church make a commitment to provide for the Christian nurture of a child. First, the parents make vows to raise the child in an environment that demonstrates values of the kingdom. And second, the members of the congregation make some commitment to nurture the child in the Christian faith. The youth minister and the youth program must never be seen as substitutes for the parents' and the church members' fulfilling their own commitments.

I remember well the first child I baptized. I was nervous, hoping I wouldn't forget anything and vaguely remembering some comment my mother had made about how easy it was for a baby's neck to break. Everything went beautifully right up to the final words of the baptism, "and of the Holy Spirit." With a sigh of relief, I said, "Let us pray." Just as I began praying, the child, whose mouth was strategically placed by my lapel microphone, began (I will not attempt to put this delicately) to throw up. Of course, this day just happened to be one of those rare occasions when the sound system was working perfectly. (I don't think the congregation heard much of my prayer.)

The parents were embarrassed and apologized profusely as they tried to wipe off my robe. But I remember thinking, *What a perfect picture of the church this is.* We are loved unconditionally by God, and God charges the community of faith to love and nurture each child in the faith whether it is easy and pleasant or not. We do not love these children and young people *because* they are cute and adorable. We love them as a demonstration of Christ's unconditional love for us.

Our goal in youth ministry is not simply to get teenagers into a relationship with Jesus Christ. We are called to make disciples—men and women who are moving toward Christian maturity and obedience. One cannot move toward Christian maturity alone. One may be able to become a mature Buddhist monk alone. One may be able to become a master in New Age religion alone. But one cannot be a mature Christian adult in isolation from other believers.

Although solitude is an important discipline of the Christian life, Christian solitude must never be confused with a concern for individualistic, private spiritual experiences. As Henri Nouwen suggests,

> Solitude in prayer is not privacy. And the differences between privacy and solitude are profound. Privacy is our attempt to insulate the self from interference; solitude leaves the company of others for a time in order to listen to them more deeply. . . . Private prayers are selfish and thin; prayer in solitude enrolls in a multi-voiced, century-layered community.[3]

Similarly, Thomas Merton said, "It is in deep solitude that I find the gentleness with which I can truly love my brothers. . . . Solitude and silence teach me to love my brothers for what they are, not what they say."[4] Our genuine experiences alone in the presence of God, then, are properly understood in the context of the community of faith.

Ideally, every young person who makes a commitment to Christ should be eager to become a part of a specific church. But the truth is that most teenagers are no more developmentally ready to make a genuine commitment to the institution of the church than they would be to make a commitment to the institution of marriage.

During the teenage years, interest in institutional religion is at its lowest. It is not so much that young people are against the institution of the church. Most simply don't care. They are at a stage of development when loyalty to relationships plays a much more significant role than loyalty to institutions.

When I was in seventh grade, I was confirmed in my church in Texas. I understood little of the commitment that I was making to God and to his people. What became clearer as I grew older was not the strength of my commitment to the church, but the strength and identity I had received because of the church's commitment to me. I stayed in the church not because I had made a genuine commitment (though I had), but because adults in the church continued to claim me even when I was an embarrassment to them.

The Christian faith becomes real to most teenagers not because of rational arguments for Christianity or because they try like crazy to hang on to what they believe, but because real people live out the gospel in what may seem to be very insignificant ways. A story is told of Bob Mitchell, the past president of Young Life, visiting with a teenager at a Young Life summer camp. This teenage boy had made a decision that weekend to follow Christ. Bob had been the speaker for that week and was eager to hear what it was that led to the boy's decision. But the boy said nothing about the content of the messages or the relevance of what he had heard. He said simply, "I guess what really did it was when you remembered my name."

If youth are not particularly interested in institutional religion, what is the use of even attempting to involve them in the church until they are older? One reason stands out: the church is the most natural context for young people to be exposed to the Christian faith and to Christian adults. These adults can introduce teenagers to Christ and to the community of faith. The community of faith is the most effective extended family for developing mature Christian adults.

Beyond the Idolatry of the Family

The most sinister idols are the good things: success, popularity, perfection, wisdom, loyalty and the like. Seeing any one of these good things as an ultimate goal can be a much more pernicious temptation for the believer than the much more obvious sins. To borrow for C. S. Lewis's vivid imagery in *The Great Divorce:* "brass is mistaken for gold more easily than clay."

As I have suggested throughout this book, the Christian family *is* God's primary tool for building faith and character in God's children, but the family is not God. Particularly now that family values are all the rage, both in the church and in the political arena, Christians must guard themselves against the temptation to idolize the family. One way to keep the value of the family in perspective is to reevaluate the commonly held hierarchy of priorities. Many teachers and leaders have listed Christian priorities in this fashion:

1. God
2. family
3. work
4. country
5. church

I wonder if this list is a biblical reflection of priorities or a cultural one. For the Christian, does the family indeed belong in second place? And does the church belong at the bottom of the list, as an optional priority "if time allows"? Or should our commitment to the extended family of the church be placed at least on a level equal to our commitment to our own families?

Though important, the preservation of the family and "family values" is not of ultimate importance for the Christian. When the family becomes the primary focus it can become an idol, as abhorrent to God as any golden calf. Our primary allegiance is to God and God alone, not to any human institution. The family is a good gift from God, an effectual means to the end of bringing glory to God. But for the Christian, nothing, no matter how noble or good, must be allowed to take the place of God or the priorities of God's kingdom.

The nuclear family is the source of our greatest joys, but it is also the source of our greatest pain and problems. I would wager that when therapists talk with deeply troubled persons, they deal with little that is not related to the nuclear family. We can be assured that in addition to any Christian values that are passed on, each nuclear family passes on its own limited perspective and unique brand of prejudice as well.

I am not advocating, though, the kind of "churchaholic" behavior that abandons family responsibilities for the sake of committee-commitment overload. I have seen fathers who would much rather attend their fathers' group than pay attention to their children. I have seen mothers who run from committee meeting to committee meeting to escape the pressures of demanding children and a mediocre marriage. And all too often pastors have allowed their marriage and family to deteriorate while they escaped into a world of ministry and programs.

Our loyalty to the church is not a tool for escaping responsibility at home. Rather, our connectedness to the community of faith is the very thing that should hold us accountable for our faithfulness to family, work and church. It is this accountability to the broader community of faith that can free us from the limited perspectives and unhealthy patterns of our family of origin.

If we will place the priority of the community of faith above the priority of our family, we will keep a stance of openness to what God may be trying to teach us, even if it goes against the grain of what we have been brought up to believe.

I know it's just youth ministry we're talking about here, but I couldn't help but bring God into it.

Implications for Ministry

1. The clearest way for a church to reflect programmatically its dependence on God's grace is to establish an intentional prayer base for the youth ministry so that each young person, each leader and each event is prayed for by members of the church on a regular basis. We do not pray because it "works" but because we understand our genuine dependence on God's grace.

2. Participation in the church's corporate worship should be modeled by the leaders, taught by the teachers and expected as normative in the growing Christian life.

3. Each church can provide regular opportunities for the youth of the church to build friendships with the pastor(s) of the church to remind them of their connection to the total church and not simply to the youth program.

Wild Hair—Invite the pastor to preach a series of sermons on the idolatry of the nuclear family and the priority of the "first family" of the Christian community.

• • • • • • • • • • • • • • • • • •

In times of change, learners inherit the earth, while the learned find themselves beautifully equipped to deal with a world that no longer exists.

ERIC HOFFER, quoted in Glenn and Nelsen, *Raising Self-Reliant Children in a Self-Indulgent World*

No one can persuade another to change. Each of us guards a gate of change that can only be opened from the inside. We cannot open the gate of another, either by argument or by emotional appeal.

MARILYN FERGUSON, quoted in Covey, *Seven Habits of Highly Effective People*

You are a Christian only so long as you constantly pose critical questions to the society you live in . . . so long as you stay unsatisfied with the status quo and keep saying that a new world is yet to come.

HENRI NOUWEN, quoted in Foster, *Money, Sex and Power*

Is it any wonder that American youth put the profession of clergy near the bottom of a list of occupations they would like to enter, ranking just a cut above undertaking?

ROBERT LAURENT, *Keeping Your Teen in Touch with God*

The Christian church is not exactly known for setting trends or embracing change.

GEORGE BARNA, *Marketing the Church*

Toto, I don't think we're in Kansas anymore.

DOROTHY, in *The Wizard of Oz*

12
Making It Work
117 Ideas for Starting a Family-Based Youth Ministry

In *chapter four I presented a primarily theoretical look at family-*based youth ministry—more of a vision than the actual building blocks. In this chapter I want to outline a number of practical ideas that can be easily implemented to get a family-based youth ministry off the ground.

What will be found in this chapter is not a collection of great new ideas, but a strategy for using many of the standard programming tools for youth ministry in a new way. I actually hesitated to include some of these ideas because they seemed so obvious, so uncreative. But hopefully, it is clear by now that family-based youth ministry is not about splashy programs or complex strategies. Its key objective (and thus the criterion for success) is simply for teenagers to make friends with Christian adults.

My experience has been that whenever a group moves from the traditional objective (collecting young bodies in a room) to the objective of helping teenagers build relationships with Christian adults, there will be resistance. Most churches hire a youth minister to build a youth "program." Quickly. Focusing on the long-term foundation is likely to be met with resistance.

The truth is that the majority of churches will simply not be able to find the kind of youth minister who can draw hundreds of teenagers to meetings. There are simply not enough of them to go around. And very few churches can afford the "Fortune 500" style of ministry. Not even those churches that can will be able to do everything the parents, the teens and the church's leadership expect. As we move into the twenty-first century, most churches will need to develop selective excellence in their youth ministries. Most churches that try to do everything will find that they end up doing very little well.

A second expectation churches should have as they begin to implement the principles of family-based youth ministry is that the normal time trying out these ideas is about three years. Some things will be a natural fit, and others will not. Quite frankly, we can expect that some programs simply won't work in some settings.

For this reason, family-based youth ministry is best begun as an "undercover" or mustard-seed kind of ministry. The great unveiling of a new family-based youth ministry would, in fact, be quite underwhelming. It would be about as exciting as watching a tree grow or uncovering the foundation of a house. In reality there is not much to see on the front end, but this "mustard seed conspiracy" will yield great returns in the long run.

I advocate that churches begin to apply these principles slowly, adding one or two ideas from each category in this chapter each year. Typically, most churches will find that the more of these events they do, the more they will want to do and the easier they will become.

I began creating family-based youth ministry programs with one rule of thumb: if it works with youth, try it with youth and parents together. Just as in youth programming, some ideas worked beautifully; others were less successful. But in general, family-based programming, used judiciously, is almost always more effective (and more fun) than having the adults and the youth apart.

In this chapter I want to present a smorgasbord of ideas to equip parents and bring families together to provide an extended family for teenagers in the church. I will present these ideas in categories of four foundational components: education, service, worship and recreation. I have also included a fifth category of "miscellaneous ideas" that don't fit neatly into one of the top four but can help a church create an intentional family-based youth ministry.

Worship

Teenagers' involvement in the worship of the church often yields more significant long-term results than does even the most active involvement in the youth program or Sunday school. For that reason alone, finding ways to involve young people and their parents in a church's life of worship is imperative.

Some churches have incredibly engaging worship services to which young people are drawn, but the average worship experience is less than compelling for most teenagers. But sitting in worship is much like having a regular place to sit at the family dinner table. Whether the food is what you would have ordered or not, you eventually grow to like it, and you know you belong.

Whether young people sit with their parents or in a youth section or the choir, their involvement in worship is crucial to their own growth toward mature Christian adulthood. It is in worship that young Christians, week after week, can offer God praise, confess their sins, hear from God's Word and offer themselves in a deeper way to serve God. It is in worship and through the sacraments of God's people that teenagers gain a sense of their connection to a rich family tradition.

Some churches have attempted to appeal to teenagers by altering their worship services, changing the style of music or increasing the variety and decreasing the length of the sermons. During my teenage years, my pastor would ask us frequently what we would like to see changed about the worship service. And to his credit, he tried almost all our ideas. But I can't say that those changes made much difference to my appreciation for worship.

The older I get, the more I see the wisdom in Søren Kierkegaard's theater analogy for worship. Although we tend to view the preacher as the performer, God as the prompter and the congregation as the audience, Kierkegaard portrayed it differently. He argued that, in genuine worship, God is the audience, the preacher is the prompter and the congregation is made up of the performers. If we simply try to "appeal" to teens by making worship easier or more entertaining, we may end up tacitly teaching them that their role in worship is to be passive spectators.

Implementing family-based youth ministry in worship is simply a matter of finding ways for teenagers to grow into meaningful involvement in the worship of the whole community. Here are a few suggestions:

1. Youth readers—Many churches have a regular tradition of using a different young person to read Scripture in each service.

2. Leading prayer—A church could invite different youth to lead the congregation in prayer during the service. Pastors could take this opportunity to work with a number of different teenagers during the year.

3. Ushers—Teenagers can work *with* the team of adult ushers on Sunday mornings, taking the collection, passing out bulletins, and so on.

4. Youth choir—Although the youth choir does isolate teenagers, it also gives them an opportunity to contribute as a group to the total church. The youth choir can also teach the entire congregation a style of worship music that is significant to the young people of the church.

5. "Adult" choir—Young people can benefit greatly from singing alongside the adults. An adult choir mentor for each teenager in the choir would be the best possible situation.

6. Sunday-school classes writing liturgy—The summer months are great times to let the teenagers pick the Scripture lessons and hymns, write the prayers and any other readings, all related to the sermon for the day.

7. Greeters—Teenagers can serve with adults in greeting people as they come to worship.

8. Minutes for missions—Teenagers can report to the congregation about their mission experiences representing the church family.

9. Youth service—Many churches set aside one Sunday or more a year for the youth to plan and lead the worship service.

10. Commissioning services—Before youth and their leaders leave for their mission trips, they can be commissioned in the church's worship service and prayed for specifically by the members of the congregation.

Mission and Service

More and more public and private schools are finding that active involvement in serving others is an important prerequisite for a complete education. More and more, the students I work with have been volunteering through their schools to work at the soup kitchen, collect toys for poor children, or any of a number of service-oriented activities.

The church doesn't need to duplicate the activities its teenagers will be involved in with other groups. The contribution that the church can make is to provide a place where youth and adult Christians work alongside each other in their volunteer service.

It is too easy for young people who grow up in churches with active youth mission programs to learn that Christian service is something *teenagers* do, something like proms and student government, and that they can expect to grow out of it. Youth-centered service events can, in fact, create passivity in teens who have learned to react by signing up for the mission project that was marketed the most effectively.

Obviously, genuine Christian service is very different from responding to calculated group motivation. Christian service is proactive, not reactive. At least part of the formula for teenagers' becoming proactive in serving is to allow our youth to see Christian adults living out their faith through service as well. Since parents are the primary faith-shapers for their children, any of the following activities will be strengthened by involving parents.

One of the problems with family-based youth ministry is that most parents think of youth ministry with the traditional model in mind. They are all in favor of their *children* doing service projects because it "builds character," but they are often less aware of their own need for a serving lifestyle. But unless the parents model this kind of behavior as normal for Christian adults, chances are that their children will grow out of the serving habit as well.

Most of the ideas that follow are simply a matter of plugging into the existing benevolent projects that a local church normally sponsors. The only distinction is that instead of encouraging adults to volunteer alone, family-based youth ministry advocates that whole families take on some of these projects together and that teenagers and adults work alongside each other.

11. Habitat work day—Most communities now have programs for building low-income housing with volunteer labor. Youth groups have been doing this kind of thing for years. It can work even better with parents involved with their teenage children.

12. Vacation Bible School—Often teenagers are recruited to lead Vacation Bible School. Why not match them up with adults in the church to lead the younger children?

13. Soup kitchen—The local soup kitchens are always looking for volunteers to serve meals. Encourage families or groups of families to sign up and work together.

14. Experience homelessness—If your church does a "Room at the Inn" type program that houses homeless people during the winter months, encourage parents (or mentors) and teenagers to spend the night together with the homeless. If your church doesn't have this kind of program, certainly some church or agency in the city does.

15. Food or care packages for the homeless—Allow groups of families to volunteer to prepare food or care packages for the homeless, or create periodic programs for adults and youth to serve together.

16. Family mission trip in the United States.

17. International mission trips—Our church sends a group of adults, youth and children to Mexico each year to build low-income housing. The children and youth seem to get much more out of the program when it is not directed at them.

18. Adopt a grandparent—Entire families (or mentor partners) could link up with an elderly person in the church or the community.

19. Visit nursing homes.

20. Weekend family mission trip.

21. Adopt international students—Every town with a college nearby is likely to have a number of international students who are in need of American friends.

22. Visit a children's hospital.

23. Sort clothes for a local clothes closet.

24. Sort food for a local food pantry.

25. Adopt a missionary (prayer, letters, financial support).

26. Participate by families in the church's fundraising efforts (Stewardship, One Great Hour of Sharing, Two Cents a Meal, etc.).

27. Deliver Meals on Wheels.

28. Find a need and meet it—In every community and church, families can come up with ways to serve an immediate need (for example, put together care packages for families of a person having transplant surgery, visit AIDS patients, reroof the youth minister's house).

Education

Typically, our Christian education activities are segregated by ages. This arrangement is efficient for the church, but in the long run it may rob young people of much-needed opportunities to learn with adult Christians.

In our church, a number of teenagers have chosen to be involved in adult Sunday-school classes. I have to admit that often their choosing not to be involved in the youth class is a bit deflating to my ego. But in my better moments, I know that what they are gaining through interaction with Christian adults is of much more value than their being a part of a well-attended youth Sunday-school class.

I am not, though, advocating that we do away with Christian education opportunities for teenagers separate from adults. As

I suggested in chapter nine, we must recognize teenagers' need to establish a faith distinct from that of their parents. My philosophy of Christian education involves a combination of teaching youth the basics of Christian literacy in creative weekly classes and offering short-term opportunities for youth and parents to learn together.

At our church, each of our six classes participates in its own three- or four-week course with parents and teenagers together. The focus of these classes is not so much informational as bridge-building, giving teens repeated opportunities to know an extended family of Christian adults. Here's how we have outlined our parent-youth courses for the year:

seventh grade—community building
eighth grade—drugs and alcohol
ninth grade—sexuality
tenth grade—communication
eleventh grade—decision-making
twelfth grade—preparing for college/adulthood

A family-based youth ministry also provides educational opportunities for parents. In research for their book *The Five Cries of Parents,* Merton and Irene Strommen asked 10,457 parents which topics they had "much interest" in learning about. Short-term courses on these types of concerns can be foundational in curriculum development for parents of youth. Seventy percent wanted to learn how to help a child develop healthy concepts of right and wrong; 60 percent, how to help a child grow in religious faith; 66 percent, about drugs; 62 percent, how to communicate better with one's children; 47 percent, effective discipline; 44 percent, more about sex education; and 42 percent, how to participate in a parent support group.[1]

A family-based youth ministry offers classes on themes related to the family for teenagers (for example, "Dealing with Your

Parents"), for parents (for example, "Understanding Your Teen-ager"), for parents and youth together, and for teenagers with other adults in the church. We have found that most effective youth curricula are easily adaptable to groups with youth and adults together.

The following list of ideas is a sampling of possible pro-grams. Most of these programs can work in various settings (for example, Sunday school, house groups, Wednesday-night programs):

29. Parent-Teenager Course (PTC) using the Serendipity Bible.

30. PTC on the basics of the Christian faith and discipleship (for example, "Bonehead Bible Course").

31. PTC using "On Line" life-skills materials (United Method-ist Publishing House).

32. PTC on sexuality.

33. PTC on drugs and alcohol.

34. PTC on music (for example, *Learn to Discern* by Bob DeMoss).

35. PTC on decision-making.

36. PTC on communication.

37. PTC on community building (Serendipity's "Begin-nings").

38. PTC on any Christian education topic.

39. Class with teenagers and grandparent-age members on any Christian education topic.

40. Movie night—Parents and teenagers watching a Christian movie together.

41. Concert—Parents and teenagers attending a Christian concert together.

42. Parenting class: *Raising Self-Reliant Children in a Self-Indul-gent World* by Glenn and Nelsen.

43. Parenting class: "Understanding Your Teenager" (Youth Specialties Seminar).

44. Parenting class: "Talking to Your Child About Sexuality."

45. Parenting class: "Youth Culture Today" (Walt Mueller, HeadFirst Ministries).

46. Parenting class: "Conflict Management in Your Home."

47. Parenting class: "Drug and Alcohol Abuse Prevention" (Community Intervention).

48. Parenting class: "Finding Mentors for Your Children."

49. Parenting class: "Parenting Adolescents" (Kevin Huggins, video series and book).

50. Parenting class: "Active Parenting of Teens" (video series).

51. Parenting class: "Building Faith in Your Family."

52. Parenting class: "What's Hot and What's Not" (panel of youth answering parents' questions).

53. Dads only class: *The Dad Difference*, Josh McDowell and Norm Wakefield.

54. Dads only class: *Ordering Your Private World*, Gordon Mac-Donald.

55. Dads only class: *Celebration of Discipline*, Richard Foster.

56. Dads only class: *The Man in the Mirror*, Patrick Morley.

57. Dads only support group—We had a group like this develop out of a Wednesday-night class for dads. This group now meets every other week for breakfast, choosing their own books to read and study.

58. Single fathers class (ideally led by a Christian single father).

59. Single fathers support group.*

60. Moms only classes, using books chosen by the mothers (for example, *Almost Thirteen* by Claudia Arp). I don't have many recommendations in this area, having never participated in a moms' group, but my wife tells me that there are

plenty of resources available.

61. Moms only support group.

62. Short-term divorce recovery course for parents.*

63. Short-term divorce recovery course for teenagers—This course could be held either in conjunction with the course for parents (as we have done in Nashville) or separately with only teenagers (Youth Specialties divorce recovery materials).

64. Support group for teenagers from divorced families.*

65. Support group for blended families.*

66. "On the Nose"—This is a fun variation of the "Newlywed Game" that lets parents and their teenage children predict how the other will answer humorous questions.

67. Pick your teacher—Let each youth Sunday-school class pick four speakers to come to their class and teach on the assigned topics for those weeks, thus exposing teenagers to a variety of adults in the church and giving the youth Sunday-school teacher a much-needed break.

68. Role-play a variety of confidentiality dilemmas.

69. Panel of experts—This idea is more of an educational method that can be used in a variety of settings. This method allows a group of teenagers, a group of parents or a group of families to serve as a "panel of experts" to respond to questions and create discussion.

70. *One on One* and *Talksheets* (Youth Specialties—both include great discussion starters for teens and their parents).

71. Lenten/Advent devotionals written by the parents or the youth.

72. PIT (Parents in Transition) seminars for parents of junior-highers, high-schoolers and collegians.[2]

*A word about support groups: Support groups for families in crisis are *not* the place to begin a family-based youth ministry. The potential volatility of these sort of situations demands that they be led by a well-trained and experienced facilitator.

Recreation

By providing our teenagers with recreational opportunities with adults in the church, we can infuse them with hopefulness and enthusiasm about becoming an adult. Often the only exposure that teenagers have to adults is as serious and didactic authorities. Many teenagers never get to laugh with adults.

We begin our Sunday-school program each week with an assembly that involves two songs, a few announcements by our resident clown and a lot of laughter. Every now and then, I see out of the corner of my eye one of the teachers eyeing his or her watch as if to say, "We've got important business to do. We can't stay here playing!"

In many ways, teaching our children to laugh with (instead of at) adults is an essential part of our curriculum. For this reason, recreation that joins parents and teenagers together is not an option but an essential for helping our teenagers grow to mature Christian adulthood.

The general principle is that almost any recreation that can be done with teenagers can also be done with teenagers and parents together. Here are just a few ideas:

73. Any parent-teen competition.
74. Volleyball.
75. Softball.
76. High ropes course.
77. Bungee jumping.
78. Bowling.
79. Snow-skiing trip.
80. Water-skiing trip.
81. Crazy games (ideas books).
82. Noncompetitive games (New Games books).

83. Bonfire.
84. A generational song exchange.
85. Hayride.
86. Dance.
87. Bike trip.
88. Superstars competition.
89. Concert.
90. Progressive dinner.
91. Picnic.
92. Capture the Flag/German Spotlight or youth group favorite game.
93. Video game night.
94. Board game night.
95. Lock-in/lock-out.
96. Cookout.
97. Talent show.
98. Rappeling.
99. Caving.

Miscellaneous Ideas

Working with the four categories of worship, missions, education and recreation is a simple way to get a family-based youth ministry off the ground. The youth minister or youth planning team can easily pick one activity from each category for the first year, in addition to one activity from the miscellaneous list below. Each year new family-based events and programs can be added and old programs revised until the church is investing as much time and energy in family-based programming as in programming geared exclusively to the teenagers.

It is important to understand that family-based youth ministry is more an attitude than a programming strategy. The following ideas are things that don't fit neatly into any of the four categories but can clearly help move a church's ministry in the direction of family-based youth ministry.

100. Parents' book table with books and other resources that can be checked out.

101. Parents' bulletin board with information about upcoming events, pictures of past events and highlights of present programs for parents.

102. Parents' newsletter—Most youth ministers send a regular newsletter to their teenagers, but very few teenagers keep calendars or newsletters! Why not send the newsletter to the parents every other month? (*Campus Life* magazine's Leader's Edition has a page in each issue that can be photocopied as a newsletter to parents of teenagers.)

103. Elder friends—Many churches have a program in which the officers of the church are matched up with young people going through confirmation.

104. Mentoring program—Interested teenagers could be matched with trained adults in the church for one-on-one friendship building over the course of the year.

105. The 70+ Club or Adopt a Grandparent—Some older adults have a tremendous ability to relate to teenagers. They also tend to have a great deal of free time! They can be used as youth leaders, Sunday-school teachers or mentors.

106. Taking parents to lunch—One youth pastor friend of mine makes it a habit to take the dads of the teenagers in the church out to lunch during the year, one at time, and to ask them to share their dreams for their son or daughter. He hasn't had a quiet lunch yet.

107. Teaching parents how to build a Christian community for their children by inviting youth leaders, pastors, missionaries and Sunday-school teachers to dinner.

108. Using parents on the youth committee—Almost every

youth ministry has an administrative committee to approve and support the direction of the program.

109. Parents' roundtable—A weekly support group for parents of teenagers.

110. Parents' committee—As a family-based youth ministry gets going, it may become helpful to develop a committee of parents to give counsel and encourage other parents' involvement.

111. Class parents—A mother or father in each class who is responsible for the planning and organization for that class's special events.

112. Parent-teen planning potlucks—We began one year with a different planning event for each grade. Parents and teenagers together planned the special events for their class for the year.

113. Annual open letter from teens to parents—By soliciting input from teens in Sunday school, the youth leader can compile a letter to all the parents from all the young people and send it out in the next newsletter.

114. Annual open letter from parents to teens—The reverse of 113.

115. Preaching on the relationship between parenting and discipleship.

116. Camping experiences—Young Life has recently developed a family camp program. Doug Burleigh, past president of Young Life, has said, "Over the years we have learned that you don't isolate a kid and minister just to him or her. Kids come in the context of families. So it makes sense to take our beautiful facility at Trail West and minister in a broader context."[3]

117. Group Magazine's *Parents of Teenagers* magazine can be a helpful resource.

As perhaps the only institution left designed and equipped to work with entire families, churches today face an unparalleled opportunity to not only reach teenagers but impact entire families. But unless we make a shift in direction, the long-term return on our investments in youth ministry will be disappointing. Those churches that choose to place their emphasis on empowering the family and the extended family of the church to do the work of youth ministry may be in for a wild ride. But the return on this kind of investment will be rich indeed.

Happy trails.

Implications for Ministry

1. After establishing a prayer team for the church's youth ministry, the first step would logically be for a team of parents and leaders to establish the priorities (for example, to increase the number of opportunities youth in our church have to build friendships with Christian adults) for the coming year and turn those priorities into specific objectives (for example, to establish a mentoring program that matches each of our young people with a Christian adult in the church).

2. Early in the first year, this planning team can pick a modest number of programs to experiment with. I recommend one idea from each of the four categories.

3. The team can expect that at least one of the ideas will not fit with the parents and youth in the particular church. Maintaining a vision for family-based youth ministry does not mean that all the programs will be successful. It does mean that the church will continue to try a variety of programs that can help the church faithfully lead young people toward mature Christian adulthood.

Wild Hair—Use Family-Based Youth Ministry *as a resource for training youth teachers, mentors, youth committee members and church leadership.*

Appendix A
A Matter of
Perspective

In *1989 my friend and mentor Robert Wolgemuth and I unwittingly* inagurated our family-based youth ministry with a four-week course for all parents and teenagers. We began the course with this skit, "A Matter of Perspective," to help parents and teenagers see the limitations of both of their perspectives.

The scene opens on Dad, driving into the school parking lot to pick up his sixteen-year-old son, Jason, after football practice.

Dad: Hey, Jas.

Jason: Hey, Dad.

Dad: Sorry I'm a little late.

Jason: It's all right.

Dad: Ya know, Jas, I've been drivin' this thing around town all day, how 'bout you drive us home?

Jason: What?

Dad: I said, would you mind driving. I've been fighting traffic all day, and I'd just as soon be a passenger and let you drive.

Jason: Yeah. Okay.

[Jason steps away from the passenger door and walks around the car. Dad slides into the passenger seat. Jason takes the wheel, starts the car, looks around to be sure it's safe to move into traffic and proceeds. After several seconds the silence is broken as Jason reaches for the radio.]

Dad: Hey, we could do without the radio.

Jason: Dad, I haven't heard anything *I* want to listen to all day. I just need to clear my mind for a minute.

Dad: [laughing] Clear your mind? With that stuff you listen to?

Jason: [lightly] Okay, Dad. Have it *your* way.

[A few more moments of silence]

Dad: Sooo, how was football practice?

Jason: Not great.

Dad: Well, didja learn anything at school today?

Jason: Daaaaad.

Dad: How 'bout Jessica? What's going on with her?

Jason: She's fine.

Dad: Are you still going steady?

Jason: Dad, we don't go *steady.* We've gone out a few times, okay?

Dad: Well, okay, whatever you call what you do. Are you still doing it?

Jason: [looks shocked] Daaaad.

[A few more moments of silence]

Dad: [takes a deep breath, trying to get something started] Hey, ya know, I was listening to a program on NPR *[Jason mouths the letters NPR]*, and they were saying that automobile accidents caused by reckless teenagers are the number one cause of death in America.

Jason: [turning toward his dad] I thought it was heart disease.

[Just then the car in front of them makes a quick stop. Dad, of course, is the first to see it.]

Dad: [putting his hand out] Whoa. Whoa, hey, Jas, careful.

Jason: Hey, Dad, don't worry about it. I saw that.

Dad: Well, it's not *you* that I'm worried about, it's all those *other* guys on the road. *[pauses]* I took that special defensive driving course last month that our Rotary Club sponsored. *[pauses]* You know, I told you about that seminar. I wish you would have come with me.

Jason: Dad, is this going to turn into another lecture?

Dad: Son, I'm just trying to communicate with you.

Jason: Daaaad.

Dad: Well, isn't that what families are supposed to do? You know, communicate?

Jason: You and I just can't seem to talk very well.

Both: [turning to the audience] We've got a problem!

*   *   *

Dr. Freud: [as if talking to Dad and Jason although facing the audience] Dad, Jason, it's not easy to admit you've got a problem, and I want you to know you've done the right thing in coming to me. Now, in order for me to help you, I need to find out what occurred yesterday after school. So Jason, why don't you go first. Just tell me in your own words exactly what happened.

*   *   *

Dad: Get in the car, boy.

Jason: Hello, Dad.

Dad: I've had a lousy day. I know I'm late. I don't want to hear anything about it. Especially the part about how on time *all* the other dads are.

Jason: Hey, no problem, Dad. I know you work hard all day long. I tried to spend the time wisely and get a little homework done.

Dad: Just a minute. *You* drive. I've been wanting to check out your driving, firsthand. This should give me a good chance.

Jason: What?

Dad: Don't act so surprised. I've heard about your driving, and I want to see it for myself. Now get over here and drive. And put on your seat belt too.

Jason: [*cheerfully*] I'd be happy to drive, Dad. [*Jason steps away from the passenger door and walks around the car. Dad slides into the passenger seat. Jason takes the wheel, starts the car, looks around to be sure it's safe to move into traffic and proceeds. After several seconds the silence is broken as Jason reaches for the radio.*] Hey, Dad, do you mind if I turn on the radio?

Dad: Forget it. We don't need to listen to that noise.

Jason: Dad, I've really had a hard day today, and I'd like to clear my mind with some good music.

Dad: Clear your mind? With that junk you listen to? Haven't you heard the stories of kids who sacrifice dogs and cats and drink their blood after listening to that music? As a matter of fact, I've read that if you listen to that stuff backwards, your mind turns to kitty litter. If I've told you once, I've told you a thousand times, a mind is a terrible thing to waste.

Jason: [*sincerely*] Well, Dad, maybe I *should* consider adjusting my listening habits.

[*A few more moments of silence*]

Dad: I guess you're ready to start in the big game Friday night. You know it's awful nice to have your dad feel good when his kid is out there on the field performing. You *know* how important it is to your mother and me to have you do well on the team. So how *was* football practice today?

Jason: Not too great. I doubt if I'll get to start, but I think Kominski probably deserves to play ahead of me anyway.

Dad: [*after a disapproving, uncomfortable silence*] Well, are you still wasting your time and my hard-earned money on this expensive private school?

Jason: Daaaaad.

Dad: And how about that girl, Jessica? Ya know, the last time I saw her she certainly was dressed suggestively. I mean, that skirt . . . and that sweater. Actually, I probably shouldn't tell you this, but from our prayer group at church I've heard stories about her mother, and you know what they say—like mother, like daughter.

Jason: Jessica's real fine, Dad. Thanks for asking.

Dad: By the way, what *do* you do on dates? Are you going steady? Have you given her your class ring? How about that ID bracelet you won at the carnival? You know, I'll bet she'd like to have that. I gave your mother *my* ID bracelet. And why don't you ever bring Jessica over to the house? You know we've got all three of those Star Wars videos. I just love the way George Mucas makes all those special effects. And *E.T.?* That Steven Spielman is such a gifted producer.

Jason: You know, we've really only gone out a couple times, Dad. And just for your information, we don't call it going steady any more.

Dad: Well, okay, whatever you call what you do. Are you still doin' it?

Jason: [understandingly] I don't think so, Dad.

[A few more moments of silence]

Dad: Speaking of drunk drivers . . . you know I've been noticing how you've been driving. I was listening to this program on NPR, and they said that teenagers today create more carnage on American highways in one week than Korea and Vietnam *combined.* They said that automobile accidents caused by reckless teenagers are the number one cause of death in America.

Jason: [turning toward his dad] I thought it was heart disease.

[Just then the car in front of them makes a quick stop. Dad, of course,

is the first to see it.]

Dad: [going berserk] Jaaaassssooooonnnn! You're going to kill us both. I'm going to die!

Jason: It's okay, Dad. I was watching. No need to get too excited.

Dad: Well, I'm concerned that all the rest of these nuts are as crazy on the road as you are. What did you do, go to Kmart to get your license? I tried to tell you that you should have gone to the Rotary Club defensive driver course last month. But nooooo, you were too busy.

Jason: Dad, if you'd like to talk about this in a civil way . . .

Dad: [interrupting through clenched teeth] I am just trying to get you to listen to me.

Jason: I'm open to that.

Dad: Don't you know that boys are supposed to respect their dads and take their advice?

Jason: I'd really like to, but sometimes it's hard to get a conversation started with you. You know, Dad, you've got a problem.

*   *   *

Dr. Freud: [talking to Dad but facing the audience] I see, very interesting . . . What's that, Dad? You want to tell it your way? Okay, if you think he missed some details, let's hear what happened from your perspective.

*   *   *

Dad: Hey, Jas. How's it goin' son?

Jason: [grunts] Humn.

Dad: Ya know, Jas, I know how much you love to drive. How 'bout you drive us home?

Jason: [grunts] Humn.

Dad: Hey, you'd be the best chauffeur I could ever have. I'm really proud of the way you've learned to be responsible behind the wheel. And I am a little tired from working hard all day to provide for my wonderful family, so I'd like to rest a little and be a passenger this time, if that's all right with you.

Jason: Uh, me? Uh, yeah, uh, okay.

[Jason steps away from the passenger door and walks around the car. Dad slides into the passenger seat. Jason takes the wheel, starts the car, puts the pedal to the floor and recklessly spins onto the access road. Dad is forced back into his seat, his head whipping back violently . . . Several seconds of silence are broken as Jason reaches for the radio. Heavy metal music blares.]

Dad: Hey, would you mind turning that down a little? It's not that I have a problem with that kind of music; it's just that I have a little headache from working so hard to provide for my wonderful family.

Jason: Shut up, Dad. It really hacks me off when you try to control my life. It's like Nazi Germany. I don't have any freedom. If you're going to make me drive, then I get to pick the music. You don't like it? You can walk. I'm just trying to clear my head, Dauhd.

Dad: Oh, I'm sorry. Does it help to clear your mind? You know, that's hard for me to understand, but I sure don't want to keep you from anything you really enjoy. I was sort of hoping we could spend some time talking. You know, sharing . . . being transparent and vulnerable.

Jason: [sarcastically] Oh, *there's* a great idea. Okay, start one up. I dare you.

[A few more minutes of silence]

Dad: Soooo, how was football practice?

Jason: [shrugging] Humn.

Dad: Anything you could tell me about your day at school that would help me understand my wonderful son?

Jason: [whining] I don't think so, Dad.

Dad: You know that Jessica certainly has an eye for bright young men. How are you feeling about her?

Jason: She's fine. I'm fine. We're fine. . . . How are you, Dad?

Dad: Do you really like her?

Jason: We've gone out three times, okay? And if you're looking to give me the third degree about what we're up to, forget it!

Dad: Well, okay. I just wanted to know if you're planning to continue your relationship.

Jason: Daaaaad.

[A few more moments of silence]

Dad: [takes a deep breath, trying to get something started] Hey, I was listening to a radio program, and they were giving some startling statistics about how innocent young people are dying in car accidents.

Jason: [glaring at his dad] It's probably more fun than having a heart attack.

[Just then the car in front of them makes a quick stop. Dad, of course, is the first to see it.]

Dad: [calmly] Son, there's a car up there that has stopped. Be careful.

Jason: Get off my back! *[The car jerks to a stop.]*

Dad: Hey, son, I know you're a good driver, it's just the other drivers I'm concerned about. I know you were real busy, but I do wish you could have come with me to the defensive driver's school that the Rotary Club sponsored last month. You know, you can never be too careful. I would sure hate for anything bad to happen to you.

Jason: [his voice sarcastically lilting] Yeah, Dad. And now you're going to tell me that you learned to drive uphill in the snow in your Volkswagen Beetle on your way to school because you were too poor to ride the bus.

Dad: Son, I do wish we had a better relationship. One where we could really communicate.

Jason: Hey, look. Our *relationship* is as good as it needs to be. None of the other kids' dads try to *communicate* with them. They just give 'em stuff and leave 'em alone.

Dad: Oh, that hurts me when I hear you talk like that. I want to have a strong, loving family. Where we really care about each other.

Jason: Look, just because you couldn't talk to your dad . . . Hey, I don't mind communicating as long as you don't expect anything out of me. Why can't you accept me like I am?

Dad: [*turning to the audience*] You've got a problem.

• • • • • • • • • • • • • • • • •

Appendix B
Has the Traditional Family Really Died?

One of the most quoted statistics about today's families is that under than 10 percent of families in America can now be defined as "traditional." In 1989, Senator Chris Dodd of Connecticut argued, "There are only one in ten American families today where you have mom at home and dad at work—only one in ten. Ozzie and Harriet . . . are gone."[1]

In a 1988 television interview, Congresswoman Pat Schroeder of Colorado asserted, "Only 7 percent" of today's families "fit the Ozzie and Harriet syndrome." In making her case for a national child-care policy, she claimed that basing such a policy on traditional families was "like saying the highway program must recognize people who don't drive."[2]

Like any compelling statistic, this one has been used by many who were obviously too busy to check the facts. The "under 10 percent" statistic is simply not true. According to a 1987 Bureau of

Labor Statistics report, traditional families (that is, father working, mother at home) account for more than one-third—the largest single category—of all families with preschool children.

Another 15.8 percent of families with preschool children can be classified as semitraditional, with the father working full-time and the mother working part-time (sometimes as little as ten hours a week). My wife, whose primary role is raising children, would not be considered as part of a traditional family because she worked one day a week doing childcare in our church's Mother's Day Out program and did some telemarketing work from our home.

When the statistics are added up, 49 percent of families with preschool children could be seen as "traditional." In other words, there is a good chance that a significant percentage of the youth we work with have grown up in a traditional family setting.

There actually seems to be a growing desire among families to return to the traditional family model. In 1986 *Newsweek* took a poll of working mothers and discovered that only 13 percent of them said they actually *wanted* to work full time. Similarly, a *Washington Post* survey indicated that 62 percent of working mothers would stay home with their children if they could afford to.[3]

In light of this reality, Steven Bayme's conclusion to *Rebuilding the Nest*, a collection of essays on the American family, offers the needed balance as we design ministries to changing families:

Stable families, in turn, both provide opportunities for personal growth and hold the key to society's future through the socialization of children. For these reasons, we should be willing to assert our cultural preference for traditional norms such as marriage and the two-parent home while at the same time accommodating and reaching out to those who have chosen to lead their lives within alternative settings.[4]

Notes

Introduction
[1] Jim Burns, *The Youth Builder* (Eugene, Ore.: Harvest House, 1988), p. 227.

Chapter 1: Something's Wrong
[1] George Barna, *Marketing the Church* (Colorado Springs: NavPress, 1988), p. 22.
[2] Michael Hirsley, "Mainline Protestants Trying to Stem Losses," *Chicago Tribune*, May 7, 1991, p. 12.
[3] William H. Willimon and Robert L. Wilson, *Rekindling the Flame: Strategies for Vital United Methodism* (Nashville: Abingdon Press, 1987), p. 42.
[4] Tom Gillespie, "The Way Back Leads Nowhere," Report of the Standing Committee on Theological Education, Address to the 200th General Assembly, *The Presbyterian Outlook*, July 18, 1988, p. 6.
[5] Milton Coalter, "Preliminary Report on the Findings of the Study of the Presbyterian Church in the 20th Century," quoted in the *General Assembly Task Force on Membership Report*, 1991, p. 10.
[6] Chart created by Duffy Robbins for presentation at the Youth Specialties National Resource Seminar, 1992, and used with permission.
[7] Mark Senter, *The Coming Revolution in Youth Ministry* (Wheaton, Ill.: Victor, 1992), p. 21.
[8] Ibid., p. 14.
[9] Mike Yaconelli, *Youth Ministry to Kids in a Post-Christian World*, 1989 Youth Specialties Resource Seminar Video (El Cajon, Calif.: Youth Specialties, 1989).

[10]Alexa Smith, "PC(USA) Educators Respond to the Study," *The Presbyterian Outlook*, April 30, 1990, p. 13.

Chapter 2: Is Anybody Out There?
[1]*Parents of Teenagers*, December/January 1990, p. 6.
[2]H. Stephen Glenn and Jane Nelsen, *Raising Self-Reliant Children in a Self-Indulgent World* (Roseville, Calif.: Prima Publishing, 1989), p. 45.
[3]Theodore R. Sizer, interview, *The Wall Street Journal*, September 11, 1992.
[4]Urie Bronfenbrenner, "The Origins of Alienation," *Scientific American* 231 (August 1974): 60.
[5]Josh McDowell and Norm Wakefield, *The Dad Difference* (San Bernardino, Calif.: Here's Life Publishers, 1989), p. 13.
[6]*Parents and Teenagers*, August/September 1988, p. 8.
[7]Andree Aelion Brooks, *Children of Fast-Track Parents* (New York: Viking Penguin, 1989), pp. 67-68.
[8]Stuart Cummings-Bond, "The One-Eared Mickey Mouse," *Youthworker*, Fall 1989, p. 76.

Chapter 3: The Developmental Disaster
[1]Andree Aelion Brooks, *Children of Fast-Track Parents* (New York: Viking Penguin, 1989), p. 179.
[2]Charles P. Warren, quoted in Kari Torjesen Malcolm, *Building Your Family to Last* (Downers Grove, Ill.: InterVarsity Press, 1987), p. 77.
[3]*TV Guide*, February 6, 1989.
[4]Neil Postman, *Amusing Ourselves to Death* (New York: Viking Penguin, 1986), pp. 60-61.
[5]From Daniel Singal, "The Other Crisis in Our Schools," *The Atlantic*, November 1991, quoted in *Reader's Digest*, April 1992, p. 112.
[6]Quoted in Charles Colson, *Against the Night* (Ann Arbor, Mich: Servant, 1989), pp. 21-22.
[7]H. Stephen Glenn and Jane Nelsen, *Raising Self-Reliant Children in a Self-Indulgent World* (Roseville, Calif.: Prima Publishing, 1989), p. 208.
[8]George Will, "Slamming the Doors," *Newsweek*, March 25, 1991, p. 65.
[9]Avery Chenoweth, "Parents Learning How to Teach Teens Meaning," *Princeton Packet*, January 12, 1983, p. 7A.

Chapter 4: It Only Makes Sense
[1]Mark Senter confirms this idea: "The high school campus has changed. No longer can people concerned with reaching youth for Jesus Christ expect to have a single program or strategy which is attractive to all of the high school population" (Mark Senter, *The Coming Revolution in Youth Ministry* [Wheaton, Ill.: Victor, 1992], p. 18). One of the keys to the success of Dan Spader's increasingly popular Sonpower model is that he has energetically advocated

reducing youth activities so that leaders will have the energy to focus their creativity on evangelism and discipleship.

[2]The only notable exception to this pattern were those young people who, although they did not connect with adults in the church, created their own adult extended Christian family by becoming ministers (including joining the staff of parachurch organizations like Young Life, Youth for Christ, Campus Crusade, InterVarsity or the Fellowship of Christian Athletes) or marrying ministers.

[3]Ben Patterson, "The Plan for a Youth Ministry Reformation," *Youthworker,* Fall 1984, p. 61.

[4]Ibid.

[5]Ibid.

[6]The Search Institute study (Peter L. Benson and Carolyn H. Elkin, *Effective Christian Education: A National Study of Protestant Congregations—a Summary Report on Faith, Loyalty and Congregational Life* [Minneapolis: Search, 1990], p. 62) indicated that only 26 percent of churches reported that parents were involved in the planning or programming of their youth ministry. The study goes on to strongly advocate that primary attention be given to the faith formation of parents.

[7]Wayne Meeks, *The First Urban Christians,* quoted in William Willimon, "The New Family," in *Peculiar Speech* (Grand Rapids, Mich.: Eerdmans, 1992), p. 118.

[8]The Search Institute study (Benson and Elkin, *Effective Christian Education,* p. 56) indicated that only 20 percent of churches have youth programs that promote this sort of intergenerational contact.

[9]Senter, *The Coming Revolution,* p. 27, describes these two organizations aptly: "Though extremely different in nature, the two organizations [FCA and YWAM] appear to have one factor in common—a well-focused target audience. Neither is attempting to be a full-service ministry."

Chapter 5: Sitting on a Gold Mine

[1]Kevin Huggins, *Parenting Adolescents* (Colorado Springs: NavPress, 1989), p. 143.

[2]Huggins's rationale for the extensive influence of parents is also instructive: "No one else (peers, teachers, even favorite recording artists) has access to a kid like parents do. . . . And exposure always breeds influence. The question many parents must ask themselves is not 'Why don't I have any influence over my teen?' but 'Why do I take so little advantage of the exposure I do have with him?' The answer to the second question is very often the answer to the first" (p. 145).

[3]Merton Strommen and Irene Strommen, *The Five Cries of Parents* (San Francisco: Harper, 1985), p. 72.

[4]Josh McDowell and Norm Wakefield, *The Dad Difference* (San Bernardino,

Calif.: Here's Life, 1989), p. 13.

[5]*Parents of Teenagers,* December/January 1990, p. 4.

[6]Andree Aelion Brooks, *Children of Fast-Track Parents* (New York: Viking Penguin, 1989), p. 88.

[7]H. Stephen Glenn and Jane Nelsen, *Raising Self-Reliant Children in a Self-Indulgent World* (Roseville, Calif.: Prima Publishing, 1989), pp. 103-4.

[8]Armand Nicholi Jr., "Changes in the American Family," *White House Paper,* October 25, 1984, p. 2.

[9]James Dobson and Gary Bauer, *Children at Risk* (Dallas: Word, 1990), pp. 167-68.

[10]Robert Laurent, *Keeping Your Teen in Touch with God* (Elgin, Ill.: David C. Cook, 1988), p. 119.

[11]Edward Hayes, *Prayers for the Domestic Church: A Handbook of Worship in the Home* (Eaton, Kans.: Forest of Peace, 1979), p. 17.

[12]Marjorie J. Thompson, *Family—the Forming Center* (Nashville: Upper Room Books, 1989), p. 23.

[13]Benjamin Keeley studied the religious behavior of both Christian and non-Christian high-school students. His study documented that young people who perceive their parents as deeply committed to their religion are significantly more religious than teens who see their parents as less committed (Laurent, *Keeping Your Teen in Touch with God,* p. 46). A 1990 *Newsweek* article entitled "The New Teens: What Makes Them Different?" explained that, in general, teenagers reflect their parents' lifestyles and values. The study found "far more congruence than conflict" between the beliefs of teenagers and their parents (*Youthworker Update,* September 1990, p. 1).

[14]Roger L. Dudley and Margaret G. Dudley, "Transmission of Religious Values from Parents to Adolescents," *Review of Religious Research,* September 1986, p. 13.

[15]Peter L. Benson and Carolyn H. Elkin, *Effective Christian Education: A National Study of Protestant Congregations—a Summary Report on Faith, Loyalty and Congregational Life* (Minneapolis: Search, 1990), p. 38.

[16]Ibid., p. 66.

[17]Quoted in Clyde A. Holbrook, *The Ethics of Jonathan Edwards: Morality and Aesthetics* (Ann Arbor: University of Michigan Press, 1973), p. 83.

Chapter 6: The Critical Care Unit

[1]Peter L. Benson and Carolyn H. Elkin, *Effective Christian Education: A National Study of Protestant Congregations—a Summary Report on Faith, Loyalty and Congregational Life* (Minneapolis: Search, 1990), p. 18.

[2]The same report confirmed that approximately 40 percent of women in their forties have a mature, integrated faith. Although the mothers appear to be much further along than the fathers, the net result is that many of the teenagers we work with do not come from a home where even one parent

models living as a mature Christian adult.
[3]Benson and Elkin, *Effective Christian Education*, p. 46.
[4]Ibid., p. 11.
[5]In the 1980s the Lutheran Church sponsored a study of family religious practices. The results showed that only 8 percent of families maintain a practice of sharing, discussing or praying together as a family (Carl Reuss, *Profiles of Lutherans*, quoted in Merton Strommen and Irene Strommen, *The Five Cries of Parents* [San Francisco: Harper, 1985], p. 134). Despite the fact that family conversations about God have a tremendous impact on the future faith maturity of children, most Christian families simply have other priorities.
[6]Strommen and Strommen, *Five Cries*, p. 129.
[7]Benson and Elkin, *Effective Christian Education*, p. 38.
[8]Ben Patterson, "The Plan for a Youth Ministry Reformation," *Youthworker,* Fall 1984, p. 45.
[9]Gordon MacDonald, *The Effective Father* (Wheaton, Ill.: Tyndale House, 1977), p. 245.
[10]David Popenoe, "Family Decline in America," in *Rebuilding the Nest: A New Commitment to the American Family,* ed. David Blankenhorn et al. (Milwaukee: Family Service America, 1990), p. 39.
[11]David Blankenhorn, introduction to *Rebuilding the Nest,* p. xiv.
[12]*The 21st Century Family, Newsweek* special edition, Winter-Spring 1990.
[13]*Saturday Review,* April 1978, quoted in Jim Burns, *The Youth Builder* (Eugene, Ore.: Harvest House, 1988), p. 35.
[14]Kevin Huggins, *Parenting Adolescents* (Colorado Springs: NavPress, 1989), p. 14.

Chapter 7: Beyond the Cleavers

[1]Edward F. Zigler and Elizabeth P. Gilman, "An Agenda for the 1990's: Supporting Families," in *Rebuilding the Nest: A New Commitment to the American Family,* ed. David Blankenhorn et al. (Milwaukee: Family Service America, 1990), p. 239.
[2]*Gentlemen's Quarterly: The American Male Opinion Index, Part 2,* 1990.
[3]H. Stephen Glenn and Jane Nelsen, *Raising Self-Reliant Children in a Self-Indulgent World* (Roseville, Calif.: Prima Publishing, 1989), p. 12.
[4]Josh McDowell and Dick Day, *Why Wait* (San Bernardino, Calif.: Here's Life, 1987) p. 65.
[5]1991 World Almanac.
[6]*The 21st Century Family, Newsweek* special edition, Winter-Spring 1990, p. 16.
[7]Marlene LeFever, "Learning," *Youthworker,* Fall 1991, p. 31.
[8]Andree Aelion Brooks, *Children of Fast-Track Parents* (New York: Viking Penguin, 1989), p. 208.
[9]Jolene L. Roehlkepartain, "When Your Ex Refuses to Pay," *Parents of Teenagers,*

August/September 1991, p. 22.

[10]David Lynn, "Research Brief," *Youthworker,* Fall 1991, p. 30.

[11]Judith Wallerstein and Sandra Blakeslee, *Second Chances* (New York: Ticknor and Fields, 1989), p. 13.

[12]*Parents of Teenagers,* February/March 1991, p. 5.

[13]*Parents of Teenagers,* August/September 1988, p. 6.

[14]*Parents of Teenagers,* August/September 1990, p. 5.

[15]One estimate suggests that women can expect to spend an average of eighteen years caring for an aging parent and raising children at the same time (Marty Fuller, "More Parents Are Feeling the Squeeze," *Parents of Teenagers,* April/May 1991, p. 9).

[16]"Growing Up Under Fire," *Newsweek,* June 10, 1991, p. 64.

[17]Louis Sullivan, *Urban Family,* Winter 1992, p. 7.

[18]*Youthworker Update,* September 1992, p. 6. Used by permission from Youth Specialties, 1224 Greenfield Drive, El Cajon, CA 92021.

[19]We would be wise to heed Lawn Griffiths's warning: "We pick up our church newsletter and program our week, like our VCR's, then wonder why people fall off the church's treadmill from exhaustion. Unwittingly, the church can undermine family life by trying to do too much for the family" (Lawn Griffiths, "When Churchgoers Are like Rats on a Treadmill," *The Tennessean,* March 1, 1992).

Chapter 8: Beyond the Teenage Family

[1]Ben Patterson, "The Plan for Youth Ministry Reformation," *Youthworker,* Fall 1984, p. 60.

[2]Earl Palmer, "Perspective," *Youthworker,* Spring 1992, p. 4.

[3]Peter L. Benson, *The Troubled Journey: Profile of American Youth* (Minneapolis: Search Institute/Lutheran Brotherhood, 1991), p. 9.

[4]Andree Aelion Brooks, *Children of Fast-Track Parents* (New York: Viking Penguin, 1989), pp. 68-69.

[5]Steven Bayme, "The Jewish Family in American Culture," in *Rebuilding the Nest: A New Commitment to the Family,* ed. David Blankenhorn et al. (Milwaukee: Family Service America, 1990), p. 153.

[6]John Guidibaldi, "The Impact of Parental Divorce on Children: Report of the National NASP Study," 1983, quoted in Merton Strommen and Irene Strommen, *The Five Cries of Parents* (San Francisco: Harper, 1985), p. 28.

[7]H. Stephen Glenn and Jane Nelsen, *Raising Self-Reliant Children in a Self-Indulgent World* (Roseville, Calif.: Prima Publishing, 1989), p. 23.

[8]Ibid., p. 19.

[9]Strommen and Strommen, *Five Cries,* p. 64.

[10]Peter L. Benson and Carolyn H. Elkin, *Effective Christian Education: A National Study of Protestant Congregations—a Summary Report on Faith, Loyalty and Congregational Life* (Minneapolis: Search, 1990), pp. 33-34.

[11] Marjorie J. Thompson, *Family—the Forming Center* (Nashville: Upper Room Books, 1989), p. 123.

[12] Benson, *The Troubled Journey*, p. 11.

Chapter 9: Walking the Tightrope

[1] Mark Senter, *The Coming Revolution in Youth Ministry* (Wheaton, Ill.: Victor, 1992), p. 177.

[2] *Journal of Research on Adolescence* 1, no. 1 (1991), quoted in *Youthworker Update*, November 11, 1991, pp. 4-5.

[3] Andree Aelion Brooks, *Children of Fast-Track Parents* (New York: Viking Penguin, 1989), p. 245.

[4] Eugene Peterson, *Growing Up with Your Teenager,* quoted in Jay Kesler and Paul Woods, *Energizing Your Teenager's Faith* (Loveland, Colo.: Group Publications, 1990), p. 24.

[5] Kevin Huggins, *Parenting Adolescents* (Colorado Springs: NavPress, 1989), p. 215.

[6] C. S. Lewis, *Miracles* (New York: Macmillan, 1947), p. 51.

[7] C. S. Lewis, *Mere Christianity* (New York: Macmillan, 1943), p. 163.

[8] H. Stephen Glenn and Jane Nelsen, *Raising Self-Reliant Children in a Self-Indulgent World* (Roseville, Calif.: Prima Publishing, 1989), p. 103.

[9] Peter L. Benson, *The Troubled Journey: Profile of American Youth* (Minneapolis: Search Institute/Lutheran Brotherhood, 1991), p. 6.

Chapter 10: A Different Gospel

[1] Robert Bellah, "The Invasion of the Money World," in *Rebuilding the Nest: A New Commitment to the Family,* ed. David Blankenhorn et al. (Milwaukee: Family Service America, 1990), p. 234.

[2] Carl Schneider, "Moral Discourse and the Transformation of American Family Law," *Michigan Law Review* 83 (1985): 1859.

[3] Chuck Colson in *Jubilee,* June 1987, p. 8.

[4] *Parents of Teenagers,* December 1990/January 1991, p. 27.

[5] *Youthworker Update,* June 1991, p. 1. Used by permission of Youth Specialties, 1224 Greenfield Drive, El Cajon, CA 92021. Taken from *Oregon Alcohol & Drug Review* 10, no. 3, in *Chemical People Newsletter,* March/April 1991.

[6] Peter L. Benson and Carolyn H. Elkin, *Effective Christian Education: A National Study of Protestant Congregations—a Summary Report on Faith, Loyalty and Congregational Life* (Minneapolis: Search, 1990), p. 23-24.

[7] *Emerging Trends,* Princeton Religion Research Center, January 1989.

[8] *Journal of Research on Adolescence* 1, no. 2 (1991), quoted in *Youthworker Update,* January 1992, p. 4. Used by permission of Youth Specialties, 1224 Greenfield Drive, El Cajon, CA 92021.

[9] James Dobson, *Preparing for Adolescence* (Ventura, Calif.: Regal Books, 1978, 1989), pp. 21-27.

[10]Henri Nouwen, *In the Name of Jesus* (New York: Crossroads, 1989), pp. 59 and 22.

Chapter 11: God Calling
[1]John Westerhoff, *Bringing Up Children in the Christian Faith* (Minneapolis: Winston, 1980), p. 7.
[2]M. Scott Peck, *The Road Less Traveled* (New York: Simon & Schuster, 1980), p. 168.
[3]Henri Nouwen in *Christianity Today*, April 5, 1985, p. 32.
[4]Thomas Merton, *The Sign of Jonas* (New York: Harcourt, Brace, 1953), p. 261.

Chapter 12: Making It Work
[1]Merton Strommen and Irene Strommen, *The Five Cries of Parents* (San Francisco: Harper, 1985), p. 191.
[2]Dave Friese, "Middle School Minister," *Youthworker,* Fall 1992, p. 11.
[3]Marge Atkinson, "Drawing Families Together," *Relationships,* Winter 1990, p. 6.

Appendix B: Has the Traditional Family Really Died?
[1]David Blankenhorn et al., eds., *Rebuilding the Nest: A New Commitment to the American Family* (Milwaukee: Family Service America, 1990), p. 11.
[2]Pat Schroeder with Andrea Camp and Robyn Lipner, *Champion of the Great American Family* (New York: Random House, 1989), p. 84.
[3]James Dobson and Gary Bauer, *Children at Risk* (Dallas: Word, 1990), p. 133.
[4]Steven Bayme in *Rebuilding the Nest,* p. 258.